Grand Brand Rajini

P. C. Balasubramanian and **Ram N. Ramakrishnan** are chartered accountants who laboriously established their respective careers outside the finance and accounting profession. They both perform business and management advisory services.

P. C. Balasubramanian is one of the founder directors of Matrix Business Services India. He is passionate about enterprise and institution-building. He is also an ardent admirer of Rajinikanth and one of the authors of the bestselling *Rajini's Punchtantra: Business and Life Management the Rajinikanth Way.*

Ram N. Ramakrishnan has worked in management consultancy for two decades. After a stint with a well-known corporate house in Mumbai, Ram set up his own consulting service and currently performs management advisory in the Arabian Gulf.

To know more about the book and the authors, visit:
- www.grandbrandrajini.com
- www.facebook.com/grandbrandrajini

Grand Brand Rajini

Brand Management the Rajinikanth Way

P. C. Balasubramanian

Ram N. Ramakrishnan

RUPA

Published in 2012 by
Rupa Publications India Pvt. Ltd.
7/16, Ansari Road, Daryaganj
New Delhi 110002

Sales centres:

Allahabad Bengaluru Chennai
Hyderabad Jaipur Kathmandu
Kolkata Mumbai

ISBN: 978-81-291-2059-5

10 9 8 7 6 5 4 3 2 1

The authors have asserted their moral right.

Typeset in Utopia Std 10.5/15

Printed at Thomson Press India Ltd., Faridabad

*We dedicate this book to the creative teams
who have conceived, developed and delivered
'Brand Rajini' to the world.
And to the 'cult of Rajini'—his followers,
fans, admirers, well-wishers across the world,
who hold him close to their hearts and
cherish the Brand Rajini experience.*

'Brand Rajini'
*We have the greatest respect and love for Mr
Rajinikanth. For the sole purposes of this book,
and to strongly establish his way of branding,
we have used terms such as 'Brand Rajini' and
'Rajini' in various places in the book.*

Contents

Introduction

A successful brand is all about what it does, not what it says or shows. It delivers consistently positive experiences to its admirers, which come from keeping its promises to them and earning their trust—that it will do its very best, at every point of contact, to deliver what is expected.

Like any person, a brand has a physical 'body'. Also, like a person, a brand has a name, a personality, character and a reputation. Like a person, you can respect, like and even love a brand. You can think of it as a deep personal friend, or merely an acquaintance. You can view it as dependable or undependable; principled or opportunistic; caring or capricious....

People have character...so do brands. A person's character flows from his or her integrity: the ability to deliver under pressure, the willingness to do what is right rather than what is expedient. You judge a person's character by his/her past performance and the way he/she thinks and acts in both good times and especially bad. The same is true of brands.

—Robert T. Blanchard,
of Procter & Gamble, in his 1999 'Parting Essay'

Here's to the crazy ones. The rebels. The troublemakers. The round pegs in the square holes. The ones who see things differently. They're not fond of rules. And they have no respect for the status quo. You can quote them, disagree with them, glorify or vilify them. About the only thing you can't do is ignore them. Because they change things. They push the human race forward. While some may see them as crazy ones, we see genius. Because the people who are crazy enough to think they can change the world are the ones who do.

—Apple Inc.,
'Think Different' ad campaign, 1997

That, to us, sums up our Grand Brand Rajini.

'Rajini' signifies a huge, respected, admired, adored, reviewed, tested, loved and even worshipped concept— it is consumed and cherished by consumers of all age groups, genders, communities and religions. Brand Rajini is, in its essence, a unique story. It is about the reaching down and pulling out of an authentic entity. To many, Brand Rajini may appear a façade; but to most, it has the power to create an almost visual connect, instantly communicating to the world the idea of a brand that delivers.

Rajinikanth the actor has outgrown his identity as a successful and talented artist: he is a superstar, a superhero, a respectable human being, a role model, or simply a 'Thalaivar' ('chief') to Indians across the globe, cutting across geographical barriers. According to Internet sources, there are over 150,000 fan clubs of Rajinikanth, not counting the Rajini websites—one of which works only when you are not connected to the Internet! The inventiveness of Brand Rajini inspires innovation in the minds of its followers too.

There is no counting the hours that admirers spend recalling their Rajinikanth rendezvous. Common sense and intuition tells us: this is Grand Brand Rajini.

For any brand to succeed, it is vital that it delight and captivate its customers. That is possible only when it finds a place in both the mind and heart of customers. Brand Rajini indeed lives in the heart, mind and souls of its hardcore fans, admirers and followers.

Did Shivaji Rao Gaikwad, the actor Rajinikanth, the superstar and cultural icon, build a brand called Rajini? Was it consciously launched? How is it still enduring? Is it merely a result of the fact that it originated in the entertainment industry? We explore these questions, and more, to find interesting parallels in the industry, cutting across borders, culture and habits, concordant with brand successes and failures that have made the branded world today.

Change, as they say, is the only constant in this world.

And Rajini has gone from lungi-clad, beedi-smoking villain to sophisticated digital robot with amazing grace— to create the world of Brand Rajini. We traverse the journey of how this brand was launched, what made it successful initially, what went into the thinking process to make it sustainable, how it tapped into the emotions of people and, finally, how it acquired cult status—giving us the conviction to conclude that Rajini is indeed one of the greatest brands to emerge out of India.

—P. C. Balasubramanian
Ram N. Ramakrishnan

1

Establishing Brand Rajini

What Is a Brand?

Take one moment and try to think about what
'brand' means to you personally. Without a doubt
certain products, brand names, logos, maybe even
jingles, pop into your head. [...] But what about
the feelings and associations connected with these
products, brands, companies? [...] A brand is an
intangible concept.

—Philip Kotler and Waldemar Pfoertsch,
in *B2B Brand Management*

Kotler and Pfoertsch go on to simplify the idea of a brand
by breaking it into four parts: 'a promise', 'a totality of
perceptions', 'a short-cut of attributes, benefits, beliefs

and values' and something that has a unique place in a customer's mind 'based on past experiences, associations and future expectations'.

While the marketing elements of a brand, such as logos and taglines, may be what come immediately to mind when one recalls the name of a brand, these are actually communication devices; it is the deeper, more intangible components that make up the overall brand personality. It is easy to equate what one sees and hears in connection with a brand with the brand itself, but it is what one feels and senses—the perception that stays in one's mind—that is the core of a brand.

The American Marketing Association defines a brand as a 'name, term, design, symbol, or any other feature that identifies one seller's good or service as distinct from those of other sellers'. But the word brand has now evolved to encompass identity: it affects the personality of a product, company or service. Brands define the perception, good or bad, that customers or prospectors sense about a product or a service.

Brand Elements

Brand consciousness may be spread through various elements that stick in the consumer's mind, making the product or service distinct and distinguishing. The continuous use of these elements helps reinforce the brand perception in the minds of its customers. A few examples of such elements that have become trademarks of particular brands:

- *Name*
  Adobe adopted its name from the Adobe Creek that ran behind the house of co-founder John Warnock. The name Adobe has now become synonymous with excellence in software for design professionals across the world.

- *Logo*
  The Nike 'swoosh' was created by Carolyn Davidson, a graphics design student at Portland University, for the Blue Riband Sports Company owned by Phil Knight. Nike adapted the logo in 1971. The swoosh today conveys the idea of superior quality when it comes to sports goods.

- *Tagline*
  The Nokia 'Connecting people' slogan was coined by Ove Strandberg and has been used since 1992. The slogan has resonance for the majority of phone users across the world.

- *Graphics*
  According to Shombit Sengupta, the founder of Shining Emotional Surplus, the four colours of the Wipro 'Rainbow flower' logo represent the four values that would provide critical benefits to end users of the company's products: human values, integrity, innovative solutions and value for money.

- *Sound*
  The famous D ♭ D ♭ G ♭ D ♭ A ♭ jingle, produced by Musikvergnuegen and written by Walter Werzowa from the Austrian 1980s sampling band Edelweiss, has been used by Intel for many years now, and perpetuates the company's perception as the leading brand when it comes to innovation in computer processors.

The Brand Personality

All brands struggle to connect with their customers. Facing stiff competition from others, brands have to battle to create customer preferences; they need to stand out and touch customer motivations. To keep them connected, brands are given a personality, the way in which they behave is planned carefully.

Human personality characteristics are assigned to a brand so that it achieves differentiation. These characteristics depict the brand behaviour that will enable the brand to take its customer relationship to a level beyond a sales transaction. For example, IBM's brand personality presents a corporate, formal, professional, somewhat stiff profile; this contrasts greatly with Apple, which depicts an individualistic, artsy, freethinker, innovative profile; versus Microsoft, which demonstrates aggressive and mainstream traits. Similarly, you have Nike, which is unabashed, empowering, achieving and winning; while MTV stands out as an expression of youth, individuality, a breaking-conventions mindset.

So, what characteristics does a brand require and how can this be built? Jennifer Aaker provided in 1997 in a paper called 'Dimensions of Brand Personality' a Brand Personality Model—an easy way to describe the profile of a brand using as analogy the personality of a human being. To describe and measure a brand personality, five core dimensions, each divided into a set of features were used. Each feature in turn was broken down into specific traits. Using this model, it became easier to measure, develop and improve the strength of a brand personality.

Jennifer Aaker proposed the following framework for a brand personality:

BRAND PERSONALITY				
Five core dimensions and their facets				
Sincerity	**Excitement**	**Competence**	**Sophistication**	**Ruggedness**
Down-to-earth	Daring	Reliable	Upper-class	Outdoorsy
Honest	Spirited	Intelligent	Charming	Tough
Wholesome	Imaginative	Successful		
Cheerful	Up-to-date			

Each facet can be further broken down into the following traits:

Facet	Traits
Down-to-earth	Down-to-earth, family-oriented, small-town
Honest	Honest, sincere, real
Wholesome	Wholesome, original
Cheerful	Cheerful, sentimental, friendly
Daring	Daring, trendy, exciting
Spirited	Spirited, cool, young
Imaginative	Imaginative, unique
Up-to-date	Up-to-date, independent, contemporary
Reliable	Reliable, hardworking, secure
Intelligent	Intelligent, technical, corporate
Successful	Successful, leader, competent
Upper-class	Upper-class, glamorous, good-looking
Charming	Charming, feminine, smooth
Outdoorsy	Outdoorsy, masculine, Western
Tough	Tough, rugged

A quick look at the core dimensions of a brand personality reveals Brand Rajini's DNA: Sincerity (to his work),

Excitement (for his fans), Competence (as an artist), Sophistication (in his style and development over time), Ruggedness (in his bearing). Drop down to the next level, and we see even more characteristics has enabled Rajini to transcend the status of a professional actor and become a brand.

A successful brand never takes its consumers or constituents for granted. It never forgets the most important promise to its constituents: what is in it for them? And when the constituents are distracted, the brand must earn their attention. The name, logo and the tagline are not the brand—a brand is ultimately an emotion, sentiment, reaction, belief, impression, sensibility and sensitivity. It has to have a human-like personality, and be delightful, charming, attractive and adorable to captivate its audience for a lifetime.

Brand Rajini

Characteristics of a brand personality alone may not perhaps justify the conversion of an actor's prowess and popularity into a brand. If we take a wide array of brand definitions and intersperse the term 'brand' with the term 'Rajini' (wherein it encompasses the various associations that the audience has with Rajinikanth), we get more insight.

'Rajini' is the essence of a unique story—a simple visual that can instantly communicate what it is about. 'Rajini' provides credibility, connects with customers emotionally, motivates a buyer and creates user loyalty.

'Rajini' is the set of expectations, memories and resolutions that, taken together, account for a decision to choose his service over another. 'Rajini' is the sum total of all experiences one has with his service. 'Rajini' is essentially a vessel for a customer's complete experience. 'Rajini' is a reason to choose. 'Rajini' is that emotional aftertaste that comes from an experience. 'Rajini' is a representation of its personality. Thus, in all senses of the terms and associations, 'Rajini' is a brand.

Without theory, experience has no meaning, one has no questions to ask, there is no learning. Theory tells us that a successful brand requires the delivery of consistently positive experiences for its constituents. To carve a niche, it requires a personality. Its customers' loyalty stems from the brand keeping promises to them, from earning their trust in the fact that it will do its best at every point of contact to deliver on what they want and expect. This trust leads to their choosing the brand time and again.

Now, think of the power of Rajinikanth's name—the punchline it delivers; the down-to-earth, honest, wholesome and cheerful sincerity that it is built upon; the daring, spirited and constantly up-to-date entertainment it provides; its charming, sophisticated, tough and rugged appeal—what you get is Brand Rajini.

Building a brand is not easy; developing and nurturing the brand is even harder. Carefully crafted strategy is at the core of all branding activities. And corporate branding has chronicled several success stories and failures. And here is a dark horse who slipped unassumingly into the celluloid world filled with icons and carved its own niche.

Brand Rajini used the actor's inherent personality strengths to develop a brand that differentiated itself from all others. It became saleable through imagination, its unique appeal and constant updating of itself. It became commercially viable with trendy, daring and exciting fare that was at the same time sincere and reliable. Rajinikanth quantum-leaped to super-stardom through wholesome, original and unique entertainment, and then evolved and acquired cult status through friendliness, humility and down-to-earth characteristics that every brand dreams of.

Brand Rajini cuts across race, religion, language, age and geography—it is analogous to the more talked about global corporate brands. The stories of highly popular corporate brands and Brand Rajini are very similar, their triumphs and disasters are not very different; the only difference is that corporate brands are more prominent, well-researched and talked about, while Brand Rajini has remained out of the limelight. This book brings to light the journey of that brand, taking the reader into the enriching, enlightening, and entertaining world of Grand Brand Rajini.

2

The Launch

Perceptions about a Brand Launch

It is a general perception that brands that have influenced people's lives came out of hype and fanfare. Most recall the brand launch event, the media blitzkrieg, the teaser campaigns, the jingles. At best, many think that the concerted plans and efforts of corporate strategists, marketing whiz-kids, brand pundits, copy writers, musicians and film makers bring about its success. Such efforts do not always go in vain. Some instances of instant success are as follow.

- In 1986, Saatchi & Saatchi formed Team One to handle marketing for the new premium brand of their client Toyota Motors. The image consulting firm Lippincott & Marguiles was hired to develop prospective names, out of which the brand Lexus was born. In 1989, Toyota carried out an extended development process, involving sixty designers, twenty-four engineering teams, 1,400 engineers, 2,300 technicians, 220 support workers, around 450 prototypes and over $1 billion in costs, to complete the project. The resulting flagship was the Lexus LS 400, which had a unique design that shared no major elements with previous Toyota vehicles. The LS 400 debuted in January 1989 and officially went on sale the following September at a network of eighty-one brand-new specialized Lexus dealerships across the United States of America. Lexus established instant customer loyalty and its debut was generally regarded as a major shock to the pedigreed luxury car makers of the world.

- A name that always pops up in the Indian brand scenario is Liril. Launched in 1975, Karen Lunal's expression of cool, tingling freshness in the waterfall, with the famous jingle tune, still lives in the minds of Indians. The bikini-clad girl under the waterfall, the feeling of exuberance from the sting of the chilled water, perfectly reflected the liberated woman. According to its creator, Alyque Padamsee, the doyen of the Indian ad world, Liril and its girl captured the average Indian woman's need for creating space for her own dreams under the shower. The famous launch quickly enabled Hindustan Lever reach the shelves across the country, making Liril the most sought after premium soap in India.

- Andersen Consulting, the professional consulting division of the accounting firm Arthur Andersen, was separated through a court ruling in August 2000 and was directed not to use the name thereafter—a name that had been built through years of toil. 'Redefined. Renamed. Reborn. 01.01.01' on a torn Andersen Consulting logo was where the rebranding and positioning effort began. Teaser campaigns were launched at the September 2000 Sydney Olympics for the upcoming brand. With the help of branding expert Landor, an internal effort named 'brandstorming' was launched with a December 2000 deadline. 'Accenture' (Accent on the Future) proposed by an Oslo employee and was selected—with a mammoth launch effort spanning 40,000 clients and prospects, 200 offices across forty-seven countries, 70,000 employees and a million new recruits—to become a name in the consulting industry.

But brands don't always emerge as champions. And launches may not always guarantee one a winning position at the podium. As Mike Tyson, the boxing champ said, 'Everybody's got plans...until they get hit'—even carefully crafted brand strategies offer no guarantee of success. For instance:

- Project Kansas was a secret project commissioned by the iconic brand Coca-Cola to test and perfect the new flavour of the famous drink—Coke. The results of test marketing revealed that the new sweet flavour was better than that of the old Coke and its primary rival Pepsi. The 'New Coke' was launched in April 1985. Within days of the launch, the company's headquarters started receiving letters expressing anger and deep disappointment over the change of Coke's original taste. Over 400,000 calls followed, averaging approximately 1,500 calls a day from irate customers. Talk show hosts and comedians mocked the change. Fidel Castro, a Coke fan, called it a sign of American capitalist decadence. An 'Old Cola Drinkers of America' group was formed to lobby Coca-Cola to either get back the old formula or sell the company. Succumbing to the backlash, Coca-Cola announced the return of the original formula in less than three months, but they called it the Coke Classic. Even then, customers were suspicious whether the old one that was being brought back was the 'true' Coke. A marketing blunder—despite all the time, effort and money spent—was set to kill the company itself.

- 'Life means more' was the tagline for an incredible ad campaign involving three of India's most charismatic and enduring icons: Sachin Tendulkar, Hrithik Roshan and Shah Rukh Khan. It saw the launch of the home-grown Indian e-commerce site Hometrade.com. The brand claimed to be the world's first FMFG (Fast Moving Financial Goods) Company, proclaiming itself the next generation in financial services. It claimed several stalwarts as its business partners: PricewaterhouseCoopers for back-office support, A. T. Kearney for strategic advice, Andersen Consulting for risk management, Dow Jones and Reuters for the latest news updates and the likes of Dun & Bradstreet as content providers. Shocked was India's financial world when Hometrade.com was discovered to be a scam. The backlash began and the company went bust almost immediately after its launch.

- Great brands launched with pomp and grandeur included Kellogg's breakfast cereal and Nestle's iced tea, but these were rejected by Indian consumers, as the products, despite their global reputation, failed to synchronize with the local cuisine and culture.

- R. J. Reynolds's 'smokeless cigarettes' tanked because everyone missed the smoke in their smoke.

- In an attempt to be the first in the category, the electronics giant Sony launched Betamax, but its demise was brought about by VHS, a competing technology.

Between these two extremes of overwhelming success and dismal failure lies the middle-stream. Most brands that have become iconic today took considerable time and effort before they began to captivate their targeted customers. Some examples of such steady development can be seen below.

- A capital of ₹15,000, a rented house-cum-office at ₹250 per month, factory space worth ₹300 and a shampoo-packing machine for ₹3,000 were all that Beauty Cosmetics had to start its business in the powerful multinational-dominated FMCG (Fast Moving Consumer Goods) market. The founder, C. K. Ranganathan, started the company in 1983 with the launch of a shampoo called Chik. Another three years on the back of a bank loan of ₹25,000 in a tight financial market, and Chik began to progress slowly. Market-innovating strategies used by the company enabled the brand to slowly push its name in the mind of the average Indian customer, who longed for a clean bath every day. By 1992, Chik was the leading shampoo in the state of Tamil Nadu. Innovation and differentiation in the shampoo business were pioneered by this little, unknown company: the concentrated shampoo sachet; the 50 ml shampoo bottle at ₹6; and the shampoo variants to satisfy local preferences in South India—reetha for Andhra, shikakai for Tamil Nadu, hibiscus for Kerala and karthika for Karnataka. The company then began an onslaught of products in the perfume, fairness and pickle market and is a multimillion-dollar business today. Under its new name, CavinKare, it is now an acknowledged game-changer in India and continues in its quest to deliver innovative products in the FMCG business.

- Detergent powder was pioneered as early as 1959 in India by Hindustan Lever. In 1969, Karsanbhai Patel, a chemist at the Gujarat Government Department of Mining and Geology, started manufacturing and packing a phosphate-free synthetic detergent powder in a 120 sq. ft area in his house. He would sell fifteen to twenty packets a day on his way to work on a bicycle. The new washing powder was priced at about a third of the more popular Surf, and the town and its customers welcomed Nirma into their households with open arms. Within a decade, Nirma had rewritten the rules of the game with its low pricing, backed by a money-back guarantee, and catapulted itself into a dominant position. To leverage its efforts to offer consumer products at an affordable price range, Nirma sought captive production plants for raw materials. This led to a backward integration programme, as part of which two state-of-the-art plants were established at Baroda and Bhavnagar. Now, in its expanded and modernized state, Nirma is a case of an Indian brand which started next-door and took on the oldest and grandest of multinational competitors.

The celluloid world is no different. Actors from 'film' families have been launched with a bang but then have disappeared with hardly a thud; actors have struggled for long to gain acceptance before they have got to a winning streak; actors have switched their images to gain popularity; actors have retired early to hold on to some measure of grace and dignity. In fact, in the film industry, failures outweigh success stories.

A company's intent is visible in every brand launch. Prima facie, target customers have to be identified, and the brand positioned for them. Immense care is taken to launch the brand: budgets are assigned, experts provide the brand's nomenclature and/or vocabulary, advertising agencies work on the brand's communications strategy across media channels, marketing, sales and distribution require scaling up, and so on. Ultimately, it is about garnering brand visibility, and a series of actions follow to grow the new brand over a period of time. Intent is also demonstrated by the company's immense faith in a brand, as continuous investments are made to retain the brand identity despite high initial cash drain.

Launches in the motion picture industry too are the same. To launch a male star, for instance, there is brand identity and positioning—as hero, villain, character actor, cameo artist, comedian, etc.—for a target audience who will contribute to the gate collections. The success of the launch depends entirely on the extent to which the brand identity is retained in the minds of the customers, who look forward to actor's next extravaganza.

Launching Brand Rajini

A closer look at the launch of Brand Rajini when introduced as Rajinikanth in the year 1975 dispels many branding perceptions. It was the era of two matinee idols in the Tamil film history holding the fort: one, MGR, the revolutionary legend; the other, Sivaji Ganesan, the acting legend. Finding space between them was indeed difficult, and marginal success was achieved by the then James Bond of Tamil cinema, Jaishankar. Alongside, a new face was emerging—with his versatility, cinematic knowledge, great dancing skills and prince-of-lovers image, Kamal Haasan was already grabbing headlines.

Enter Brand Rajini—called 'Shruti Betham' ('wrong tune' or 'cacophony' in Tamil), in a small yet significant role that turns the tide of the movie *Apoorva Raagangal*.

It was the period when movies in colour caught the consumer's eye, but the creator, K. Balachander, opted for black and white, depicting his protégé in black. Shabbily dressed in tattered clothing, of average height and with a thin physical frame, no linguistic background in Tamil—this was the first visual. The creator, his master, perhaps chose him because of his eyes, which he said spoke a million languages. The character was introduced to disrupt the happiness of a young hero who was waiting to rescue his damsel in distress. The brand adopted a legendary name—that of an upright lawyer, Rajinikanth, portrayed brilliantly by Sivaji Ganesan in Vietnam Veedu Sundaram's 1973 magnum opus *Gauravam*.

Brands, actors or roles are conceived for an audience, but Rajinikanth had none. He came, we saw and he did not conquer. The movie won many laurels: for the acting prowess of the young hero (Kamal Haasan), the beauty of the elder heroine (the late Srividya), the precociousness of her daughter (Jayasudha), and the title song ('Ezhu Swarangalil—Vani Jayaram') won a National Award. But Rajinikanth just cleared the stile as yet another actor knocking on the doors of the film world.

Even the smallest of brands is introduced to the world with at least some ballyhoo. But Brand Rajini did not have the luxury of a big launch—or even a launch. He was branded neither a hero nor a villain, nor even a character artist. His first appearance on the silver screen lasted only a few minutes. The brand had no identity and it did not have any target customers in mind. In the film, Rajinikanth walks onscreen to open the gates in wide-angle—this was perhaps the only indication that a new brand was walking in to be a game-changer.

Fate could have made Rajinikanth an eternal character artist, at best in a supporting role, but it was written otherwise. Critics ignored him and most others decided to wait and watch. Nevertheless, it set some curious and creative minds to work, for it—Brand Rajini—was unique.

- It was of a different complexion;
- It was not traditionally attractive;
- It was not conventional;
- It was new to the consuming community;
- It did not use its own name but an adopted one (of an already established, unforgettable character);
- It launched without any fanfare and co-existed with established, recognizable brands-in-the-making;
- It did not have an identity of its own;
- The target market was not clear at the time of the launch.

Cornerstones of Brand Rajini's Launch and Initial Foray: Differentiate and Dominate

For most of the consumers of Rajini, the name is a synonym for differentiation. Rajini walked the talk. And he prudently performed so as to not clone or copy the revolutionary, the acting legend or the emerging icon— establishing individuality was at the nucleus of his work. Speed was the name of his game. And he gradually gained mastery over dialogue delivery. Armed with these traits, Rajini pronounced differentiation rather loudly, for he approached with the same characteristics a different set of roles in successive films. His histrionics were questioned by his critics but perhaps made them detached watchers and progressively converted them to ultimately becoming his admirers.

Rajini's successive films were all about differentiation: the taming of the adamant and villainous son (*Moondru Mudichu*), the sadistic husband who deserved to be stoned (*Avargal*), the simple, ethical and sacrificing friend, without his usual negative traits (*Bhuvana Oru Kelvi Kuri*), the arrogant village thug who is stoned to death (*16 Vayathinile*), and the unscrupulous and perverted villain (*Gayathri*). He was neither the archetypal hero nor the regular villain, but he converted his limitations into strengths to build a strong identity as a differentiator.

Brand Rajini probably knew that this was the only trick up its sleeve to stand up to the competition. Differentiation was the clincher that enabled Rajini to launch his brand of histrionics. Great differentiators can similarly be found in the branded world.

Rajini became an admirable bad guy onscreen and there were immense positive results to the negative roles he played. He perhaps received the most applause for every first entry into the film as a villain—a phenomenon new to the industry, at least in the southern part of the country.

Consider, now, the examples of some global brands— the way they started, immediately differentiating themselves, and continued to grow.

- The iconic brand Nike's first products were running shoes based on the 'waffle design sole'. Their differentiation factor lay in the shoes built for sports—track and field, baseball, ice hockey, tennis, association football (soccer), lacrosse, basketball and now cricket. From Nike Air Max to the Nike 6.0, Nike NYX and Nike SB shoes (designed for skateboarding) and cricket shoes called Air Zoom Yorker (designed to be thirty per cent lighter than their competitors), it was all about differentiation. Air Jordan XX3, a high-performance basketball shoe, was designed with the environment in mind. Nike recently teamed up with Apple Inc. to produce Nike+, a product that monitors a runner's performance via a radio device in the shoe that links to the iPod or iPhone.

- Apple's initial foray into the world of computers was the personal computer Lisa and then the Apple

Macintosh that created a new wave in desktop publishing. Apple continued differentiating with various products—the iPod, iPhone, Apple TV and iPad. The world watches Apple Inc. for its next wave of differentiation.

- IKEA sold household furniture but with a difference. Their stores were large, coloured in the Swedish blue-and-yellow, and had 'one long natural way', where consumers could see exactly how the furniture would look in their homes. They started their first store in 1953; ten years later, they opened their next store outside Sweden, in nearby Norway. Today, IKEA has stores in twenty-five countries, the latest being in the Dominican Republic. The company is now all set to launch its stores in India.

- Pears differentiated with a transparent soap as early as 1789. It produced the soap using a completely different methodology from other existing soaps. According to Unilever records, Pears Soap was the world's first registered brand and is therefore the world's oldest continuously existing brand.

As Howard Schultz, the CEO of Starbucks says, 'A great brand raises the bar—it adds a greater sense of purpose to the experience'. Same was the case for the brands mentioned above, including Brand Rajini.

Brand Rajini Narrows Focus

Brand Rajini's differentiation and characteristic traits became an attraction for the consumers. Brand Rajini now realized that style and substance were the core strengths that needed to be kept in focus. Focus enables a brand to avoid being all things to all people and keeps the consumer engaged in a specific manner.

Brand Rajini then began an aggressive movement to dominate the battle turf. As far as style and substance went, Brand Rajini wanted to be the leader. Coupling the speed of dialogue delivery with the already established characteristics, Brand Rajini gradually enhanced its dare-devil image in the minds of the consumers—they now looked forward to the next move, which always overwhelmed them when it came.

A distinct quality of any respectable brand is that it signifies trust—and hence it is the duty of the brand to live up to expectations. Brand Rajini did so. Soon Brand Rajini's focused style became the talk of the town. In dark alleys and unoccupied rooms, fans tried to emulate elements of that style: the twist of the glasses, the chucking of the cigarette to the lips, the lighting of the matchstick using only one hand. Most failed, but some succeeded in mastering the moves and presented them in front of their friends, with the characteristic punchline: 'How is it?' ('Ithu eppadi irukku?') At the very least, one could mime offering Chiclets a la Rajini. Brand Rajini consumers did not seek any other alternatives—they had found 'style'.

This was what the narrowed focus of Brand Rajini helped it to accomplish—to hook consumers in a way and for a style statement that was not to be found anywhere else. Similarly, for other global brands, narrowed focus helped them to establish themselves strongly.

- Starbucks narrowed its focus from the regular coffee shop in the US (where one finds soup, salad, sandwiches, burgers, hot-dogs, muffins, cake, ice-cream and coffee) to simply brewed coffee. The first store operated at 2000 Western Avenue, Seattle, for nearly five years, and then moved to 1912 Pike Place, where it operates even today. Coffee drinking became a major trend via the Starbucks cafes. Today, there are over 17,000 cafes across fifty-five countries, and Starbucks's primary focus continues to be coffee.

- Subway narrowed its focus from the abundant delicatessen (where one finds almost anything for the customer on the go—sandwiches, chips, roasts, chocolates, cakes, toffees, coffee, beverages, cigarettes and newspapers, etc.) to the submarine sandwich. Offering multiple bread choices and ingredients, Subway became a specialist sandwich maker, a brand with a focused product to offer.

- Toys 'R' Us was initially a children's supermarket, but it narrowed its focus to selling only toys. It has been in business for sixty years and has become a global brand; it is considered the last word in toys when it comes to an extensive assortment of new toys, old favourites and great value, for generations of parents and kids alike.

Films Have a Shelf Life, But Brand Rajini Had to Live On in the Minds of Consumers

The differentiation trait in Brand Rajini made a mark and the focus on the core strength of style raised anticipation amidst audiences. The challenge of every brand is to create a huge perceived difference between the particular brand and its competitors in the minds of consumers, inspiring passion for the brand. The different roles, each delivered in a unique manner, laid the founding stone for establishing Brand Rajini. Listed below are some of the signature gestures and scenes that contributed to the growth of Brand Rajini.

The Rajini Rendezvous

Film	Signature
Apoorva Raagangal	The laughter of a person dying when he is offered money to keep away from his estranged lover, saying that all he wants is forgiveness.
Moondru Mudichu	The oft-repeated 'Theek hai'; the swift move of the cigarette from the hand to the mouth.
Avargal	The flick of the glasses; the ultimate expression of being 'the most hated'—a stone thrown at his face by a street urchin.

16 Vayathinele	The imagination of the street ruffian in seeing the heroine's mother in her daughter's outfit and his questioning of the handicapped simpleton on his daily chores—both ending with the famous remark 'Ithu eppadi irukku?' ('How is it?')
Gaayathri	The way he slaps the security guard as he goes past him, returns, puts the lit cigarette to the guard's mouth and tells him not to repeat his folly.
Aadu Puli Aattam	Shaving himself as he rides his bike, reflecting the attitude of the villain.
Bhuvana Oru Kelvi Kuri	The flicking of cigarette ash with the snap of his fingers as he sings 'Raja enbar manthiri enbaar.'
Bairavi	The poster depicting him with a snake in one hand while he pats it with the other.
Aval Appadithan	The natural way he explains to his friend that there is nothing called love and it is all lust.
Ilamai Oonjaladukirathu	The emphasis on style from the word go—signing with a pen modelled on the transistor aerial; the walk up the stairs, walk back and walk forward; the catchphrase 'Chiclets?'
Mullum Malarum	The anger, anguish and hatred, all at once, when he says 'Ketta paya, sir...Kaali' ('A bad guy, sir...this Kaali') to his boss.

Ninaithale Inikkum	A full-fledged comedy role: when he asks his girlfriend if she fell for his style, haircut or smartness and she says it was for his beard, a disappointed Rajini removes the beard and says 'Inthaa vechhukko' ('You can keep it'); the ever-popular remark 'Shiva Sambo'.
Dharma Yuddam	The movement of the glasses in his hand as he sings 'Aagaya gangai'; smoking while singing a song; swiftly moving from the rear of the car to the front when speed matters; hitting goondas with a cricket bat like he is thumping leather.
Naan Vazhavaippen	'Michael D'Souza, a true Christian'—his way of introducing himself; taking out a cigarette from his jacket pocket when everyone thinks it will be a pistol.

It is indeed strange that no one wanted to emulate Rajini's looks, his wardrobe or his haircut—people simply wanted to either repeat his actions or use his style to emphasise their points of view. Rajini leapfrogged this concept of inculcating style into every action onscreen and came up with path-breaking scenes that captivated his audience. The brand was well on its way to engulfing the minds of its favoured consumers, and more and more people were being attracted by its magnetic pull.

Brand Rajini's Emotional Connect

Rajini began the emotional connect with customers—his fans. Tamilians are sometimes extremely vociferous about their emotions when it comes to film stars, sportspersons, politicians and other celebrities. Their adulation for Rajini was no different. Apart from capturing the audience with his differentiation and uniqueness, he also enraptured them with stellar performances early in his career.

In *Bhuvana Oru Kelvi Kuri*, he enacted, without displaying his unique traits, the role of a loser; but he was a winner with the audience. Pitted against another legend, Kamal Haasan in *Ilamai Oonjaladukirathu*, he played a sincere and sacrificing friend but with trendy style and mannerisms. In *Mullum Malarum,* he was the loving brother, the angry worker and despondent physically challenged person rolled into one.

Intriguingly, in this film, Brand Rajini was perceived as poaching in the territory of the acting legend Sivaji Ganesan, who had produced and acted in an unforgettable brother-sister-relationship movie called *Pasamalar*; Rajini's role was compared to his. In his forty-ninth movie, *Naan Vazhavaippaen*, Rajini shared the screen with the legend—and the media reported that Rajini overshadowed him. Rajini, with all humility, rejected all this brouhaha and requested that he never be compared with the legend.

When his fifty-first movie, *Aarilirunthu Arubathu Varai*, was launched, the audience was stunned to see an aged Rajini on screen, a struggling lower-middle-class worker with a simple heart—there were no histrionics. Sivaji had been known for brilliant portrayals in exceptional roles as an aged man in his youth. And in a carefully crafted role, Rajini too performed with grace and sincerity. Sivaji's fans could have rejected and demolished him as their legend's imitator or competitor, but in Rajini they perhaps saw a genuine effort to simply be a good actor. Rajini had turned the legend's fans into his own. Women thronged the cinema halls and a new segment of loyal customers was added to Brand Rajini's consumer group. The brand, in one stroke, had conquered the hearts of at least half of the Tamil cine audience.

It is interesting to draw another parallel. Sandow M. M. A. Chinnappa Thevar, originally a stuntman, became a producer with his own brand of pot-boiler, feel-good, commercial stunt movies, which had one common hero—the revolutionary legend MGR. Thevar decided to launch *Thai Meethu Sathiyam* with Rajini—in a traditional MGR-ish themed story about a son's love, respect and responsibility towards his mother. The movie was also a kind of rehash of a hunter's role in a cowboy outfit enacted by MGR in the mega-hit *Vettaikaran* produced by Thevar.

Brand Rajini was now in a sticky wicket of sorts, for another comparison media salvo was in the offing. Perhaps it was Rajini's authenticity, commitment to work and his brand of professionalism in the industry that resulted in MGR blessing him; the actor predicted to Thevar that Rajini was going to soon emerge as the leading star of Tamil cinema. *Thai Meethu Sathiyam*, despite the *Vettaikaran*-ish role, captured the hearts of the rest of Tamil cinema's audience.

The fan clubs that were split between the two legends, Sivaji Ganesan and MGR, now had a common friend. Brand Rajini won the war but without a battle. With acceptance from both sides of the coin, there was no need for a toss. And from there onwards, there was no stopping Brand Rajini.

- Read this company's mission statement: 'We fulfil dreams through the experience of motorcycling, by providing to motorcyclists and to the general public an expanding line of motorcycles...' Think motorcycles, and you connect immediately with Harley-Davidson. Think Harley, and you see the image of a cool dude riding the quintessential highway cruiser. Say Harley, and you hear the vroom of its engine. Smell Harley, and you feel a whiff of petrol and leather. You can emote with Harley: if you are not a motorcyclist, you may hate Harley, fear it or treat it with disgust; if you are a motorcyclist and don't have a Harley, you envy the next one you see; if you are a Harley owner, you feel gratification, perhaps even arrogance. That is the emotional connect of the brand. It conquers logic.

- Why are the users of this next company's products so loyal? Why do they always stick to that kind of technology? Why do they have an overwhelming presence in everything they do? Is this a tech company or a marketing company? It's neither;

it's a brand—and its name is Apple. The power of Apple's brand keeps it alive: it differentiates, it fails, it resurrects, it imagines and it innovates. Apple has established a deep, lasting bond with its customers. It's an iconic brand. Even more, an emotional brand—its customers just love Apple. Its connection with customers transcends commerce. Apple has established around its products communities that are people driven—bringing an emotional experience to computing. Apple does not sell products any more; it sells the brand, evoking in people's minds a mix of hopes, dreams and aspirations.

It is this kind of connect that Brand Rajini has established with its consumers. Rajini's admirers do not go to watch just the movies—they go to watch Rajini himself. Brand Rajini sells itself—the products are secondary to the brand.

Brand Rajini Was All about Confidence, Guts and Seizing Opportunities

'Carpe diem' ('seize the day') was the central theme behind the Brand Rajini launch. It was all about grabbing small opportunities that came along instead of waiting for one big one. The confidence of bringing about a differentiation in the market, however small, is where the Brand Rajini story began.

Confidence is also about guts. Rajini was not petrified at the thought of showcasing his skills alongside the greats legends who ruled (or were about to rule) the film world. His initial foray as a guest artist, playing the second fiddle, the character artist and even tertiary roles in films, speaks of Brand Rajini's confidence, guts and the seizing of opportunities.

Similar attributes have been demonstrated by other brands across the world, and their stories easily validate the points under discussion.

- In 1887, a sixteen-year-old boy from Sweden left his home for the promise of America, with only five dollars to his name and unable to speak a word of English. This boy's name was John W. Nordstrom. The early years were tough for the young immigrant; he laboured in mines and logging camps just to survive. But Nordstrom persisted and kept taking on manual labour jobs. After struggling for ten years, the twenty-six-year-old Nordstrom picked up the daily newspaper to find that gold had been discovered in Alaska. After two years of hard labour, navigating and surviving in difficult terrains and relentless competition, Nordstrom was able to save nearly $13,000. He then moved to Seattle, to invest his small fortune in 1901 in his first shoe store, just fourteen years after coming to America. Through the twentieth century, Nordstrom's empire grew from the one shoe store in downtown Seattle to what is now a multibillion-dollar retail empire. But for that confidence, attitude, optimism and guts when starting out, Nordstrom would have never been a name today.

- In the spring of 1891, twenty-nine-year-old William Wrigley Jr moved from Philadelphia to Chicago, with only thirty-two dollars to his name. Soon after arriving, Wrigley began selling soap and, as an incentive to customers, if they purchased his soap he would give them a free can of baking powder. Soon baking powder proved to be more popular than the soap, he was selling; so Wrigley switched his business. A year later, in 1892, Wrigley used chewing gum as an incentive for buying his baking powder. Again, chewing gum proved to be more popular than baking powder. And so he switched his business again. The first brand of chewing gum Wrigley produced was Juicy Fruit in 1893. Through his own personal hard work as a salesman and his ability to advertise, Juicy Fruit soon became the top-selling chewing gum in the country. Wrigley has since then has seen ups and downs in the market, but has remained a staple— and perhaps the most visible brand—in the chewing gum business, even journeying into the twenty-first century in the same position.

- 1984 was the time when Indians were looking out for the world's motorcycles to invade their homeland. Suzuki was the first mover, with Honda, Yamaha and Kawasaki coming in rapid succession. Honda bikes were associated with their racing background— the engine capacity, style and modern technology. However, Honda, in India, decided to cash in on the Indian mindset: 'Average kya hai?'—the scenario in which KMPL (kilometres per litre) rules over KMPH (kilometres per hour). Seizing the opportunity, Honda introduced a four-stroke engine bike, the CD100, which talked only of its fuel efficiency—a whopping eighty kilometres to the litre. Honda completely changed its image in India from 'style' to 'efficiency'—an impressive show of confidence and guts in deviating so far from what had been previously seen as its primary appeal. Very soon, Honda became the number one bike seller in India—you had to just 'Fill it, shut it and forget it'.

Brand Rajini's Strength at Launch: Experience and Credence

Brands require 'search attributes'—the evaluation that can be made prior to the purchase either through the brand name or the price. They require 'experience attributes', which can be evaluated only after purchase or during consumption. And finally, they require 'credence attributes', something that cannot be determined even after purchase or consumption.

Brand Rajini stood as testimony to a true brand: the evaluations came from the audience, who chose his films. As the scenes progressed, as the dialogues were delivered, as the eyes focused on the gestures—Brand Rajini guaranteed a variety of experience. But the added advantage offered at its launch was the brand's 'credence'. People who watched Rajini came out thinking about him. Word about him spread, his actions were revisited and tried out. Rajini's audience enhanced his credence by emulation and by the consistent expectation of 'more' to create even more gratifying audience experiences—and every single time, Brand Rajini delivered. The name, the experience and the credence is what brand value is all about.

- Travelling abroad to receive medical treatment—and that too to a developing country? But the cardiologist Dr Prathap C. Reddy's vision was exemplary as he opened India's first for-profit hospital in southern India, in Chennai in 1983. Critics harped on the concept at a time when medical treatment for both specialized fields and cash-rich patients was moving towards the West. Infrastructure was dismal in India, but Dr Reddy counted on the inherent strengths and the quality of Indian doctors, their diagnostic abilities and, of course, the price that it all came for. To the world, Apollo was a shock. But Apollo offered top Indian medical professionals the opportunity to treat the world's patients; and to the world, it offered top-class service and treatment at a very affordable cost. Apollo built its search, experience and credence attributes through its quality service. Its credence grew initially in the UK market, and then extended to other countries. Needless to say, Apollo has by now traversed along the world to build renowned top-class medical facilities in many countries outside India.

- 'We think the need is for starting from scratch on virgin land and building a community that will become a prototype for the future.' With that, Walt Disney directed the purchase of forty-three square miles of virgin land—twice the size of Manhattan Island—in the centre of the state of Florida. There, he master-planned a whole new Disney world of entertainment, which included a new theme park, motel-hotel-resort vacation centre and his Experimental Prototype Community of Tomorrow (EPCOT). After more than seven years of planning and preparation, including fifty-two months of actual construction, Walt Disney World opened to the public, as scheduled, on 1 October 1971. Epcot Center opened on 1 October 1982. Certainly, Disney had already had its search and experience attributes, but with the Florida Disney World, Walt Disney became a legend and a folk hero, his name representing imagination, optimism, self-made success. His credence grew, as a man who always did his best to touch the hearts, minds and emotions of millions across the world.

Brand Rajini Learnt from Its Competition

Brands need not copy others, but they can emulate and be inspired by their competitors. Brand Rajini did the same. Whilst essentially keeping away from any of the factors that made the iconic legends who they were at the time of its launch, Brand Rajini certainly learnt from them. The acting legend Sivaji had a lot of struggle in his history; he achieved success in the film world after a series of travails in the arena of theatre. The revolutionary legend MGR's first screen appearance was in *Sathi Leelavathi*, which was released in 1935, and it took over a dozen years of persistence before he achieved a big breakthrough with *Manthiri Kumari*. The emerging legend Kamal Haasan had gone through a continued search for excellence in different domains of film making—choreography, photography, assistant direction, guest roles, playing character artists and villains—before finally becoming a hero.

Brand Rajini knew from the start that the path to glory was strewn with thorns. And Brand Rajini's greatest strength lay in its ordinary making—in Rajini's the extraordinary determination and his ability to learn from others, and package and adapt those qualities as his strengths.

- The mechanical watch pioneered in India by HMT was very much a part of the middle-class Indian's life. But the Tatas came in as a game-changer, with the Titan brand of quartz watches. The Tatas learnt from their competition that the best strategy was to beat them at the core: with a new mechanism altogether, and stepping away from the heaviness of steel watches. The Titan watch mechanism had a quartz model and the designs were dramatically different from everything available in India. Soon they innovated further by going digital altogether. Exquisite style and up-to-date technical innovations helped Titan capture the younger market very easily. Titan's watches became more than mere timepieces—they were statements of style, objects that were coveted.

- In January 1984, Michael Dell decided to go out on a limb based on his conviction that there was enormous potential for cost savings in a manufacturer selling PCs directly instead of the conventional indirect retail channel in practice. In January 1984, Dell registered his company as PC's Limited, operating out of a condominium. In May, Dell incorporated the company as Dell Computer Corporation and relocated it to a business centre in North Austin. The dorm-room headquartered company sold IBM PC-compatible computers built from stock components. The company employed a few order takers, a few more people to fulfil them and, as Dell recalled, a manufacturing staff 'consisting of three guys with screwdrivers sitting at six-foot tables'. The venture's capitalization cost was $1,000. In 1985, the company produced the first computer of its own design, the Turbo PC, which sold for $795. Dell advertised its systems in national computer magazines for sale directly to consumers and custom-assembled each ordered unit according to a selection of options. The company grossed more than $73 million in its first year of operation. Dell was a clear example of how it learnt from the competitors to win the game, beating them in their own turf.

Validating the Brand Rajini Launch

The launch of Brand Rajini proffers a mixed bag when compared to traditional brand planning. To start with, it had no competitive terms of reference—the set of customers as the target market, the nature of competition associated with the target market and brand positioning. But it did have one sole objective—finding a distinct place in the minds of its customers. The cine world, both in terms of producers and consumers, was divided equally then, through their allegiance to the two legends. Risks were already being taken with the emerging third legend and there was the belief that there was no space for anyone else. Yet, Rajini epitomized two pertinent brand launch attributes.

First, the brand stood out in terms of Points of Difference (POD)—traits that consumers could strongly associate with Rajini's brand of acting, positively evaluate and could not find the same in another existing brand in the film industry. Brand Rajini's POD was that it was desirable, it differentiated and it delivered.

Brand Rajini also came untouched in terms of Points of Parity (POP)—attributes that were not unique to Rajinikanth but were comparable with other brands—a credible, legitimate form of entertainment was offered.

The third important facet for a brand launch is the 'brand mantra', which articulates the heart and soul of the brand—a short, three-to-five-word phrase that captures the spirit of the brand. Brand Rajini had no brand mantra, but coming from the film industry, the key dialogues delivered in his films assumed the place of Brand Rajini's mantra.

Brand management tells us how important these three attributes are in making a mark in the positioning and launch of a brand. Brand Rajini thus validates brand theory, with the success of the launch through sufficient POD and POP attributes that appealed both to the head and heart of the consumer.

Brand Rajini was now on the runway, ready to take off.

The Brand Rajini Launch—Takeaways

Don't create hype	Brand Rajini would have been a disaster if Rajini's debut had been announced as the arrival of the next superstar or the next style king or the next action hero. He was none of these in his first, second, third or even his fifth film. Reflect the brand through its actions.
Don't clone rivals	Brand Rajini did not attempt to imitate or clone the senior legends or the emerging ones, even though it learnt from them. A brand has to be original in all respects.
Go for what you know	The power of Brand Rajini was in its style and substance. Everything else was treated as peripheral. A brand should portray only what it is capable of.

Avoid customer confusion	Brand Rajini raised the bar for his customers' expectations with focus and without misleading them. A brand has to stay simple in order to invade the consumer's mind and not compound it with confusing messages.

3

The Rajini Resonance: An Emerging Brand

The Case for Brand Resonance

A brand evolves throughout its life cycle. At first it emerges as a relevant new presence in the competitive marketplace, characterized by its fast growth in five to ten years. Many brands fail during this stage, and continuing to be a winner is a challenge. The brand can also 'hit the wall' at this stage, when it is unable to take the critical step of transforming and leveraging itself into a sustainable entity. The brand then transforms and proliferates; it makes the leap to get into a leading position. This can last from ten to thirty years and is possibly the best time for the brand. The brand then reaches the 'dominate' stage, which is its ultimate goal, but there is also the fear of stagnation. And finally the brand reaches the 'reinvention' stage, when it reengineers itself even if everyone thinks it is fading into the landscape.

Professor Kevin Lay Keller of the Tuck School of Business, Dartmouth College, describes in his book *Brand Planning* what is required for moving up the brand value chain. He propounds four essential building blocks to avoid the 'hit the wall' syndrome, enabling the brand to emerge a winner. The building blocks are defined as:

- *Brand salience:* how often and how easily is the brand brought to the customer's mind;
- *Brand meaning:* the performance and the image of the brand in the minds of its consumers;
- *Brand response:* the personal connection, feelings and opinions of the consumers;
- *Brand resonance:* the quality, the character, the timbre, the reverberation of the brand in the minds of its consumers.

Consider the following example.

- In 1905, Hans Wilsdorf and his brother-in-law Alfred Davis founded Wilsdorf and Davis in London. The company name Rolex was registered on 15 November 1915. The company won loyal customers through its continued differentiators: the first waterproof wristwatch (Oyster); the first wristwatch with an automatically changing date on the dial; the first wristwatch with an automatically changing day and date on the dial (Rolex Day-Date); the first wristwatch case that was waterproof upto 100 metres (330 feet); the first wristwatch to show two time zones at once; the first watchmaker to earn chronometer certification for a wristwatch. The first self-winding Rolex wristwatch (called the Bubbleback because of its large case-back), powered by an internal mechanism that used the movement of the wearer's arm, was offered to the public in 1931. In 1968, Rolex collaborated with a consortium of sixteen Swiss watch manufacturers to develop the Beta 21 quartz movement used in the Rolex Quartz Date. Rolex produced specific models suitable for extremes of deep-sea diving, mountain climbing and aviation. Early sports models included the Rolex Submariner and the Rolex Oyster Perpetual Date Sea Dweller. The latter watch had a helium release valve, co-invented with Swiss watchmaker Doxa, to release helium gas build-up during decompression. Rolex is the largest manufacturer of Swiss-made certified chronometers. To date, Rolex still holds the record for the most certified chronometer movements in the category of wristwatches.

Rolex is an excellent example of a brand launched, and then moving to the emerging and leading brand phases. It is still the most commonly recalled watch brand, serves a niche customer base, performs well because of its distinct components and materials, attributes a high-profile image to the wearer, is symbolic of success and wealth, provides ultimate quality levels, is always innovative in design and has extreme repeat-customer loyalty.

Brand Rajini's start-up efforts had great concordance with an emerging brand's characteristics.

- *Salience*: in the competitive celluloid world, where the latest film makes or breaks a career, Rajini stood out with consistent variety.
- *Performance*: a Rajini film was assured of outstanding performance, whether the role played was simple, intense, brave, or anything else.
- *Image:* the style and mannerisms caught the customers' eyes, was registered and emulated by them, and induced greater expectations from the brand.
- *Feelings, responses, judgements:* Brand Rajini set up a winning streak for the investors in commercial terms, yet the distinctive style and display of histrionics made the experience enjoyable for viewers as well; Brand Rajini emerged as a 'win-win' for all.
- *Resonance:* Brand Rajini had its own set of customers thronging the cinema halls to catch a glimpse of his next reverberations.

Brand Rajini Emerges on the Basis of Presence, Not Publicity

Despite acting in movies in 1975 and 1976, Rajini did not have the comfort of brilliant advertising. It was more word-of-mouth, sometimes just a reference. The fundamental thing about building a brand is a deep understanding of the customer—leading to fresher ideas and more potent creativity—that ultimately makes the brand a winner. Publicity is a great tool, but it does not assure customer purchase preference until the brand performs. Performance has to be across a wide spectrum so that the brand's presence is observed, its use or service realized and customer satisfaction derived. Publicity for a brand is a great facilitator, but the driver is the brand itself.

Brand Rajini took off in the initial years by creating a presence. By 1979, Rajini had acted in a whopping fifty-three movies, averaging more than ten movies a year; 1978 was a blockbuster year when he managed to do twenty movies. Rajini's reach extended beyond the borders of Tamil Nadu and into Karnataka (ten Kannada movies), Andhra (nine Telugu movies) and Kerala (one Malayalam movie). As any good brand manager, Brand Rajini focused on one region initially, while at the same time test-running the brand (as a new product under the same brand name) in other regions. Through this all, the differentiation factor was evident in all the movies and the focus on style and substance continued.

Similar brand extension behaviour has been practised by many other successful brands.

- Body Shop was set up by Anita Roddick in the UK in 1976. It expanded annually by fifty per cent. Its shares were floated in UK's unlisted securities market in 1984. When it was listed in the UK stock exchange, it was nicknamed 'The shares that defy gravity' because its price had increased by five times. In 2006, it was sold to L'Oreal for £652 million, fetching Anita Roddick £130 million.

- Walmart was founded by Sam Walton in July 1962 in Arkansas, USA. Within five years, the company had expanded to twenty-four stores across Arkansas. By 1970, it had thirty-eight stores in operation, with 1,500 employees and revenues of $44 million. It was listed in the New York Stock Exchange in 1970. By 1975, Walmart was operating 125 stores, with 7,500 employees and sales estimated at $340 million. By the time of its twenty-fifth anniversary, Walmart had 1,198 stores, with sales of $15 billion and 200,000 employees.

- Infosys started with its flagship delivery centre in Bangalore in 1992, with 160,000 sq. ft to house 1,000 employees. Mangalore, Pune, Chennai and Mysore centres emerged in rapid succession, with Mysore as the core training centre. The company built a centre in Bhubaneswar in 1997, in Thiruvananthapuram in 2001, and continued further expansion. Today, the Infosys brand supports an eighty-one-acre campus at Bangalore, and the company has built over 28 million sq. ft of infrastructure facilities to house over 125,000 employees.

What is remarkable is that the advertising budgets of the above-mentioned companies continue to remain relatively low despite them being very successful brands. In the same way that these established entities relied on their delivery rather than publicity, Brand Rajini depended entirely on itself for sustenance.

Brand Rajini Gains Visibility

Brand visibility refers to a brand's ability to gain the attention of its target audience. As several brands compete for the attention of the consumer, the brand that offers them the best value will succeed in its efforts. It is the brand which has the ability to gain prominence, satisfy customer needs and generate a level of comfort and satisfaction that earns preferred status.

This cannot be done easily unless the primary task of brand visibility is achieved. The right kind of visibility is a boon and poor/misplaced visibility is a bane—this axiom applies to all products, professionals, politicians and performers, including actors. Onscreen, the actor needs to get the right visibility and steal it to capture the attention of the audience; off-screen, the actor needs to be in the news, in the right kind of situation—and always about something interesting.

How did Brand Rajini accomplish this over the years? Let us take a look.

The Rajini Rendezvous

Film	Signature
Aarilirunthu Arabathu Varai	Not displaying any of his differentiating traits in a single instance!
Billa	The suave don in the remake of *Don*: 'My name is Billa.'
Johnny	The stylish barber and the miser who counts his roses before he plucks one for his lover.
Naan Potta Saval	Labelled 'Super Star' in the credits, even though he was not one then; the song 'Nenjae un asai yenna' still motivates many like MGR's song 'Unnai arinthaal, nee unnai arinthaal'.
Murattu Kalai	The rustic, dhoti-clad, simple farmer with a ferocious roar: 'Seeviduven!' ('I will chop your head off!')
Netrikkan	The interrogation of his wife: question-slap-request, question-slap-request, repeatedly, until she surrenders the truth; 'Chakravarthidaa' (I am the king').
Thillu Mullu	The interview; losing one of his greatest assets—his moustache; the spotting of the double in the football stadium; entering his boss's house disguised as his twin; the romantic interlude 'Ragangal padinaaru'.
Moondru Mugam	The arrogant, tough Alex Pandian walking onto the screen: 'Sheela, Sheela, Sheela'; kicking away the chair as the local goonda is about to sit on it.
Thambikku Entha Ooru	The stylized walk, with his hands in his pockets; his body language as he sings 'Kaathalin deepam onru'; further adventures with snakes.

Andha Kanoon	Surprising his fans with his fluent Hindi; sharing the screen with his role model, the iconic Amitabh Bachchan.
Sri Raghavendra	His 100th movie; playing the role of his guru, whom he worships every day.
Bloodstone	First appearance in a full-fledged English movie; both role and film were insignificant, but it was a milestone for the brand.
Rajathi Raja	A brand new image, new style and a makeover; 'Malayala karai oram' still lingers in the ears and the heart.
Raja Chinna Roja	The first Indian film to use animated characters with actors; wins the hearts of kids and they are added to his fan base.

Some image building to generate curiosity about 'What are you up to?' is also a good strategy. A brand's image forms part of its core, so the question of what it intends to do is critical.

Brand Rajini was a scene stealer from the word go when it came to visibility. Even in scenes where actors have to be inactive, while others are doing their bit, Rajini used different tactics to get noticed and grab attention. There was no debate over whether it was important or relevant; at the end of the day, Brand Rajini wanted to gain attention. And the fact was that when Rajini drew the audience's attention, attention was withdrawn from substantially from his co-stars.

It was not unusual to find the audience focusing on Rajini while the heroine was sweating it out with difficult dance steps, emotional outbursts or a prolonged monologue; Rajini always had something going on in tandem—a flick of his wrist, a swish of his hair, a peculiar handling of a nearby object or just a chuckle. He, simply put, grabbed attention. People have often commented that when they were with Rajini at any point of time they felt that he was the one who was grabbing the limelight, be it on or off-screen. Power brands command that kind of respect and attention.

Visualize a retail shelf packed with many FMCG products. From shampoo to shaving cream, from beverages to beauty products, from skin care products to biscuits—visibility plays an important role for a brand or product to capture the consumer's attention, and this holds good even for established brands. Just like packaging, size, colour, message, POS (Point of Sale) materials, visibility via large volumes is extremely important to gain attention. This is one of the important ways in which relatively new brands are slowly and surely established amidst power brands in the same category.

Visibility enables brand recall. And brand visibility is about creating a buzz that it is more likely to be retained in the mind of a customer, in the right place and at the right time. A good product at the wrong forum or at an inappropriate time would not produce the desired results; whereas, the right visibility can catapult a relative newcomer into a position of immense popularity and recall value.

- Oral-B spent years developing a new kind of manual toothbrush that would produce clinically significant benefits beyond any other brush. Oral-B CrossAction was the first manual toothbrush designed to enhance brush performance. Fully appreciative of the uniqueness of this brush, the company set about defining a new premium category of toothbrushes, setting it apart from the other toothbrushes found on the shelves of retailers. A different set of aisle displays was used in shops to gain visibility: one set of display-adaptors with three dozen toothbrushes, another with twelve dozens. Large floor stickers with the caption 'Removes more plaque than any other toothbrush' were used. Every shopping cart carried the same advertisement as the floor sticker, grabbing the attention of every consumer who made contact with the store. In-aisle ads were placed, pointing out the new toothbrush product category. The advertising effort was consistent across all media: 'More Angles, More Action, More Effective.' Oral-B's success and breakthrough in a saturated toothbrush market was substantially aided by a clear visibility strategy.

Brand Rajini in the News

A new brand should be able to create favourable news in the marketplace. Whenever a new brand emerges, there is a strong correlation between the brand's success and the buzz around it—what's new, what's hot, what's current.

Actors are no different: if you have to get attention, be in the news. Essentially, the brand has to make the transition from being a news seeker to being the news maker. As the saying goes, there is no business like show business—and Brand Rajini was part of that show.

Brand Rajini was frequently in the news. Initially, it was regarding Rajini's origins: his tryst with the transport department as a bus conductor, his struggles to fund his training at a film institute, his days of wandering while he sought opportunities in films.

Soon, there was nothing left to report about Brand Rajini's background; the focus then turned to Rajini's character—his habits, his vices, his professionalism, his commitment, his respect for his mentor, his house, his cooperation with co-actors.

Following this, Brand Rajini sought proactive publicity to facilitate brand positioning—his every new move began to make the news. And he began to make moves that were guaranteed to draw media attention—a look at the table above provides ample evidence of the same.

Some instances of proactive publicity used by various brands can be seen below.

- Alfred Hitchcock floated a dummy of himself in the Thames to generate publicity frenzy for his film *Frenzy*.

- When Southwest Airlines launched direct flights to Memphis, it invited Elvis impersonators to make the first journey. The ensuing images of 200 Elvis lookalikes arriving at Memphis, slightly worse for the wear, guaranteed headlines for Southwest, a differentiating airline.

- EasyJet invested a large portion of its marketing dollars in a lawsuit against the Dutch Airline KLM, claiming unfair competitive practices, thus positioning itself as the underdog on the side of the public.

- Trivial Pursuit marketers sent game samples to celebrities featured in the game and radio personalities who had an affinity for trivia.

- A non-profit organization whose mission was to encourage women over forty to get annual mammograms wanted a message that would 'break through'. Outdoor signs featuring a bare-chested woman with a double mastectomy were posted along major highways, with eye-grabbing copy such as 'Over 40? Don't wait until it is too late. Get a mammogram today' or 'Which pain is worse? Over 40? Get a mammogram today'.

It is often said the publicity is considered the more able and effective force in branding; people tend to read more when it comes to publicity articles compared to copy-written or well-choreographed advertisements.

Brand Rajini 'Hits the Wall' But Bounces Back

One of the trappings of success is criticism. Success also brings detractors. The years 1979 and 1980 were tough for Rajini. Popularity is a dangerous disease, especially when it attacks an ordinary human being. The volume of films, the strong, continuing adulation, the fan-frenzy, coupled with non-stop work, indulgence in newfound wealth and a host of such circumstances—Brand Rajini was going through a very rough patch.

Rajinikanth was declared by the media to be in a critical health situation, more mental than physical. Brand Rajini, they concluded, had commenced writing its obituary. The film folk dismissed Rajini as well, reporting incidences of non-cooperation that disturbed directors and producers. There were reports of violent incidents too. Suddenly, Brand Rajini was in the news for the wrong reasons.

But Rajini's creator, K. Balachander, was steadfast in his belief in the brand and stood by the actor. He pleaded with the film folk and media to not write him off. He stated with immense faith and confidence that such talent was rarely born, and the artist had to be saved from his crises.

However, it is pertinent to note that the brand performance between 1978 and 1980 showed no sign of deterioration: Rajini's performance was getting more powerful, aggressive and versatile, along with the retention of his natural style and mannerisms.

Enter *Dharma Yuddam* ('The War for Dharma'). The audience was torn between the gloom of impending failure of their favourite star as reported in the media and the high expectations of his continuing brilliant efforts on the screen as they walked into the theatre, first-day, first show. As the audience prayed for their idol to recover his stance and stature, Brand Rajini bounced back: the war for dharma was his victory. He proved with his performance that he was not a 'podi dappa' ('snuff box') as he is called by the heroine in the film. He was careful, full of poise and gentlemanly, without surrendering his typical traits and mannerisms—and his efforts in the movie set aside all the wrong notions that were pervading the industry and the media. His use of the cricket bat to beat the villains at the climax was greeted in the same way that people greet a cricketing hero thumping a ball all the way to the boundary line.

Brand Rajini was not alone in the branded world in this instance of spectacular recovery. There are many renowned brands which re-rose like a phoenix from its ashes, coming back with a bang from what people considered the last stages of the brand's life.

- Nintendo was a huge success on its launch in 1985. But as competition grew, with the upsurge of Microsoft's Xbox and Sony's PlayStation, Nintendo lagged behind, confused about how to stay relevant in the super-competitive gaming market. Finally, Nintendo brought its brand back to the forefront with a radical new addition to the gaming industry: the Wii. With the Wii Fit, Nintendo intelligently added an element of physical activity to a pastime that was generally pitted at couch potatoes. The Wii also added an element of family-friendly social interaction to the video game experience—thus creating a whole new audience in the world of video gaming.

- The Mini Cooper was fading into history before it was discontinued in 2000. BMW re-released the car in 2001, with a similar exterior but an improved interior. The new Mini became instantly trendy, offering a retro effect and experience that consumers immediately fell for. In an era when fuel economy was the topmost concern for most car owners, the Mini resurrected its status as a popular and trendy car and, with the association with the BMW name, it was now also considered a luxury brand.

- Perhaps the only brand associated with an aftershave used to be Old Spice. However, with time, the brand began to lose its appeal for younger consumers: men with six-pack abs and a carefree, sporty outlook considered Old Spice suited their fathers and grandfathers, not themselves. Unable to relate itself to the new generation, Old Spice soon vanished. But on 14 July 2010, Old Spice resurfaced with the fastest growing online viral video campaign ever, garnering 6.7 million views after twenty-four hours, ballooning to over 23 million views after thirty-six hours. Old Spice's agency created a bathroom set in Portland, Oregon, and had their TV commercial star, Isaiah Mustafa, respond to 186 online comments and request on websites like Twitter, Facebook, and so on—the Old Spice man even proposed via a YouTube video to a woman on behalf of one of the viewers. With sales increasing by 107% within a month, Old Spice was back in the reckoning.

Brand Rajini Was about Authenticity

A litmus test for a brand's success is its claim to authenticity. Authenticity begets integrity. Integrity is all about ethical conduct and stems from genuineness and transparency. From the word go, Brand Rajini did not seek publicity through 'stunts'; every style statement and mannerism was integrated as part of the actor's personality, and nothing was a 'gimmick'. Professionalism was the brand's bread and butter. Brand Rajini also allowed other brands to exist and grow alongside, never usurping their work for prominence. And it never attempted to clone its rivals and struggled at all touch-points to retain originality.

Rajini was brutally honest about his background and his lifestyle, which was previously unheard of in the industry. The media hunted for dirt in his life and background but found nothing—Rajini himself disclosed all details about himself, fully affirming the brand's status as genuine and its stake to authenticity. The trust and confidence that Brand Rajini inspired was thanks not only to its performance and newsworthiness but also its attempts to close all gaps in public perception.

When Coca-Cola says 'It's the real thing', customers

perceive it as genuine and are convinced that it is indeed the real thing—everything else is a poor substitute. When the Tata Group says that substantial portions of its equity stakeholders are charitable trusts, people do not question it simply because it comes from the Tatas. Taglines of leading brands—such as 'America's favourite ketchup' (Heinz), 'The King of Beers' (Budweiser), 'It's everywhere you want to be' (Visa), 'The Citi never sleeps'(Citibank), 'Just do it' (Nike)—are just not taglines but statements of authenticity.

No brand can become a star by accident; this stardom stems from intention, sincere effort, intelligent direction, skilful execution and authenticity—it is because the brand represents a wise choice amongst many alternatives that people choose it.

Rajini the Emerging Brand—Takeaways

Don't price too high	Despite being an emerging star, with commercial success for all his producers, Brand Rajini did not 'cash in'; Rajini was never billed as a star who made a killing when it came to money. Bad pricing and high pricing can result in the death of a good brand.
Be the best in your area of focus	Rajini, through the volume of movies, continued to remain the best in his area of focus: differentiating style and substance. Brands should never get overwhelmed by their success; they should stick to what made them acceptable to the consumers.

Bigger isn't always better	Big banners and producers figured in Brand Rajini's movie list, but not always; Rajini spread his success among both small-time and big-time labels.
	Brands can continue to perform well in a small way rather than attempting too many big things too early.
Don't become a stereotype	Rajini never fell into the stereotype trap that was so convenient for emerging stars; although falling in the category of a commercially successful brand, the variety of roles was what acted as the spice for his fans.
	Brands should continue to innovate and inspire their consumers, else they will get buried.
Improve on the original	Brand Rajini had its string of failures, the ups and downs, just like any other brand; but Rajini excelled in improving on the original: if one traces his performance in every movie in his repertoire, the graph shows an ascending straight line.
	Brands should transcend their original shape and bring in new experiences for their loyal consumers.
Don't do it alone; walk with others and let them in	The hallmark of Brand Rajini was that it coexisted and cooperated with other brands and, when necessary, allowed them to have their deserved public attention.
	Co-branding increases the probability of premium pricing, deters copying and combines different perceptions of individual brands with a single product.

4

Brand Rajini: The Making of a Power Brand

Managing Brands for the Long Term

Life becomes difficult when you get to the top. A small wrong move can pull you down. Inconsistency in delivery can make the brand lose customers. Insufficient supplies can frustrate them. Customer preferences change over time. New customers flood the market with different tastes and preferences, dispelling 'the old is gold' mantra. But the brand's legacy cannot be ignored. The image, the innovation, differentiation, inspiration, effort and consistency that made the brand engrave a permanent place in the minds of its consumers have to be sustained even in changing times. An emerging brand has to get to the next level, to a status of power, and that needs strategic long-term thought and action.

Let us consider some other brands.

- Established by two IITians, Sachin Bansal and Binny Bansal, who worked for Amazon.com, Flipkart.com commenced operations, replicating the Amazon model, in 2007. Initially launching their business through word-of-mouth, today Flipkart is the largest online bookseller in India. By 2010, the business broke even and has since witnessed a 100% growth quarter by quarter. The business diversified from books to selling CDs, DVDs, mobile phones, cameras, computers, office supplies, electronics, home appliances, kitchenware, personal care gadgets and healthcare products. Employing more than 5,000 people now, the business has expanded with support from owner funding, venture capital funding and a spate of acquisitions, starting from ₹4 crores in 2008-09 to nearly ₹500 crores today. The company assures delivery through its eight delivery centres across India. The brand is now powerful in India, but what next? How will Flipkart.com sustain its onslaught on the e-retailing scene with the arrival of giants like Amazon.com in India? How will it fund its expanding business? Sustaining its growth in the long term will be Flipkart's greatest challenge.

- Tractors and jeeps are now part of this company's legendary products. Viewed as a conservative sleeping conglomerate in the 1980s, Mahindra & Mahindra (M&M) broke every rule in the book with its growth strategy. Diversification saw M&M move away from its core auto sector as it built businesses in various other domains. And then it happened with a bang—M&M captured the heart and soul of the urban Indian with its Scorpio SUV. With the more famous imported SUVs out of reach for the new-age Indian, Scorpio appeared as a blessing with its value offering. The Scorpio changed along with the times, with engine upgrades and face-lifts; it now offers a suite of options from a basic model to an automatic 4X4. M&M in the meantime also enhanced its older utility vehicle, the Bolero, to make it the largest selling utility vehicle in India. M&M today is a power to reckon with; it has the highest sales for utility and sports utility vehicles in the country. Then the XUV 500 was launched to brilliantly capture the changing mindset of the consumer who preferred a cross-breed or a crossover. The XUV 500 came with all the frills and whistles of a luxury car for a value-for-money pricing that made buyers throng M&M's showrooms with their chequebooks. With limited production capacity to meet the unprecedented demand, M&M stopped their order booking and moved to a lottery system of allotment that upset many; the XUV 500 is now a high-demand but limited-production vehicle. What will M&M do now? How will it retain its initial aura, sustain the consumer demand, ensure that they don't turn away towards competitor offerings that are planned to enter the market soon? Their best brains must be at the table, chartering the key strategies.

Brand gurus have advocated many ideas that ensure the retention of brand value or equity in the long term.

- Strategic actions revolve around what the brand represents, what it supplies, the needs it satisfies, how it ensures that its products are superior and strong.

- Brands also need to ensure that favourable and unique associations continue to exist in the customers' minds.

- Brands have to be revitalized; the breadth and depth of brand recall for the customer need to be increased; the brand's strength and its distinct image have to be enhanced.

- The quantity (how much?) and the frequency (how often?) of delivery need to be built up.

- Customers are vulnerable and need to be retained: old customers may be lost and have to be recaptured, neglected segments have to be addressed and new-age customers have to be brought into the fold.

- A corporate image is also a good strategy, with a variety of products under the umbrella name, with different brand positioning and continued brand enhancements.

Numerous and varied are the strategic ideas and every company carves a niche through its distinct approaches and actions. Brand Rajini too had its own ideas. And in its actions, the hallmarks of a power brand can be seen.

Brand Rajini: The Archetype

Brand Rajini's objective was to continually grab attention, to never leave the minds of the consumers. Unconsciously, Brand Rajini chose to be 'the archetype'—universally familiar characteristics that transcend time, place, culture, gender and age. Brand Rajini represented eternal truth, utilizing roles and storylines that regularly appear in our mythology, fairy tales, literature and classic films to tap deep into the emotions of people. Brand Rajini was not always the 'champion', a character which usually fights for truth, defends the weak, challenges unjust systems, fights the bully and rescues people in distress.

Margaret Mark and Carol S. Pearson, in their 2001 book *The Hero and the Outlaw*, advocated the theory of building extraordinary brands through the power of archetypes. Brand Rajini used a similar idea almost two decades before to ensure consumer retention. By using different archetype models that were familiar to the customers' psyche, Brand Rajini ensured it remained at the top end of the customers' preference spectrum. Brand Rajini being in the entertainment industry was a blessing, for it enabled the delivery of a range of archetypes on the path to becoming a power to reckon with. An assortment of Brand Rajini 'archetype roles', which raised his status to that of a power brand, can be seen below.

The Brand Rajini Rendezvous: Archetypes

THE MAVERIC (rebel, outlaw, rogue)	
Goal	Freedom from the established norms; defy, disobey and non-conform
Brands	Virgin, Harley Davidson
BRAND RAJINI	BILLA
THE EVERYMAN (good boy, average Joe)	
Goal	Bonding with everyone; humble, hardworking and friendly
Brands	Walmart, Visa
BRAND RAJINI	THILLU MULLU
THE INNOCENT (saint, angel)	
Goal	To achieve a simple and pure life; doing the right thing
Brands	IKEA, Google
BRAND RAJINI	SRI RAGHAVENDRA
THE ENTERTAINER (performer, jester)	
Goal	Using humour and fun to make friends
Brands	Budweiser, Fanta
BRAND RAJINI	THAMBIKKU ENTHA OORU, GURU SISHYAN
THE VILLAIN (bad, ugly)	
Goal	Satisfying passions through whatever means necessary
Brands	Onida (using the devil's image for the 'Owner's Pride, Neighbour's Envy' campaign)
BRAND RAJINI	AVARGAL, MOONDRU MUDICHU
THE INTELLECTUAL (genius, expert)	
Goal	To find the truth through diligence
Brands	CNN, MIT, Wiki
BRAND RAJINI	JOHNNY

THE SENSUALIST (pleasure seeker)	
Goal	Seeking perfect enjoyment through physical experience
Brands	BMW, Cadbury
BRAND RAJINI	NETRIKKAN
THE SERVANT (martyr, slave, monk)	
Goal	To provide service to others
Brands	Red Cross, Amnesty International
BRAND RAJINI	AARILIRUNTHU ARABATHU VARAI,
THE TRADIONALIST (old-school, conservative)	
Goal	Prospering through old-fashioned values
Brands	Old Spice
BRAND RAJINI	ENGEYO KETTA KURAL

Brand Rajini was also a nurturer (like Volvo), a connector (like Facebook), an artist (like Adobe), a ruler (like Microsoft), an explorer (like Jeep/Scorpio/Safari) and, finally, a simple thrill-seeker and achiever (like Nike/Adidas).

Brand Rajini Maintained Relevance

David Aaker, in his book *Brand Relevance: Making the Competitor Irrelevant* (2011), advocates that brands achieve real growth by developing innovative offerings, which create 'new categories' or 'subcategories'. This essentially makes competitors irrelevant because they lack the distinct features or benefits, enabling the brand to win the brand relevance competition. Brand Rajini did not get into proclaiming that its brand of films was the best; instead it created a new category for itself.

The revolutionary legend MGR had branched into politics and governance, the acting legend Sivaji Ganesan was entering his twilight years and the emerging legend was outlining his own path of creating role-based films to improve his quality and genre. This resulted in a gap in the customer's search for pure entertainment. A number of actors made films in that decade to recapture the histrionic qualities of the erstwhile heroes, but Brand Rajini chose to create a 'wholesome entertainment' category of films.

Once Brand Rajini took up the challenge of creating that category, it conceived the concept and executed it with innovative roles. With this, continued loyalty was ensured. The brand encouraged customers to think and select the category. When one wanted a wholesome entertainment experience, one selected Rajini. As the films released and the brand's loyalty factor increased, Brand Rajini effectively closed doors for any competitor to try and usurp that position in the marketplace. At best, you could only make a good copy.

Consider the following case studies.

- Think of a hybrid car—a new category whose unique characteristic is its low fuel consumption and low emission—and what you get is Prius. The NHW10 model was launched in 1997 in Japan. NHW11 launched in America with more power that satisfied the higher-speed and long-distance-travel requirements of the American drive. In 2004, the

Prius was redesigned completely as a mid-sized lift-back, and led to 530 patents for the vehicle. It used an all-electric AC compressor for cooling and a smaller and lighter NiMH battery with warranties for 240,000 kilometres or ten years. The Prius was a SULEV—a Super Ultra Low Emission Vehicle—and was certified an advanced technology partial zero emission vehicle. The new Prius debuted in 2010, with an estimated mileage of 4.7 litres for every 100 kilometres. Thanks to its electric water pump, Prius had the first consumer auto engine that required no accessory belts. Prius used a new range of plant-derived ecological bioplastics, made out of cellulose derived from wood or grass instead of petroleum. There are others who make hybrids, but Toyota created that new category, which had immense relevance given the rising fuel prices across the globe, and the next available hybrid is only the next best.

- Roy Raymond, a Stanford Business School graduate, felt embarrassed trying to purchase lingerie in an open departmental store. He opened the first Victoria's Secret store in 1977, exclusively for lingerie, in Palo Alto, following with a mail-order catalogue business. Victoria's Secret stores created a comfortable environment for men, with wood-panelled walls and helpful sales staff, in order to buy lingerie for women. Instead of racks and racks of lingerie hanging to be picked up after checking the size, Victoria's Secret displayed single styles, paired together and mounted on wall frames. Men could conveniently browse for styles for women and sales staff would help them with their purchase from the inventory at the back office. In 1990, although Roy Raymond sold the company, the brand was left unchanged because of its special category creation, yielding $1 billion in revenue—the largest lingerie retailer in the world.

Brand Rajini Ensured Sufficient Supplies

What is the point of a brand claiming to be at the top of the heap when consumers are not supported and supplemented by proper supplies in sufficient quantities in the relevant markets? Front-end supply chain management is a challenge even for the best brands as they need to ensure sufficient availability on the limited retail shelves. Consumers need to increase their consumption and at the same maintain the frequency of consumption so that the usage and brand awareness remains intact. This holds good for an actor on the silver screen as well. Talent, capability, acceptance, promos are all relevant and important, but unless these are supported with quality and quantity (powerful roles and larger numbers of movies), the actor may fail to get noticed adequately.

A gruelling 128 films in a span of fifteen years (that is, almost eight films a year from 1975) is a mammoth effort from an individual given the complexities of film making. But that was what made Brand Rajini a power to reckon with. And Rajini completed another twenty-two films to deliver the targeted 150th film by 1990. There was enough and more for the audience to continuously savour Brand Rajini's spice and flavour. Rajini's repertoire was not restricted to Tamil films alone; it continuously extended to Telugu, Kannada and Hindi, along with one Bengali film (*Bhagya Devata*). Sufficient supplies for a powerful brand lie not only in the numbers but also the consistent quality that they come with.

- If you are looking for a city which is a brand, look no further than the entertainment capital of the world—Las Vegas. What made this city into a rarefied class of its own that lured customers year after year from the turn of the twentieth century? Rare for a city, it enjoys a brand image that no city can copy. From any number of perspectives—fun-filled entertainment, gambling, fine-dining, shows, even notoriety—there is no dearth to its appeal. How does Las Vegas do this? It continuously supplies an abundant variety of entertainment outlets with quality—it is the best when it comes to hospitality, dining, art-on-display, shopping and spectator extravaganza. A continuous media blitzkrieg keeps alive the urge to head to Las Vegas when you have the money and are in the mood to indulge. Every time you visit Vegas, you see something new that others haven't, and the story continues. There is no one who regrets his or her Vegas trip, and everyone wants to go there. Other places that you can go to are only imitations of the Las Vegas experience. The Las Vegas catchphrase—'What happens in Vegas, stays in Vegas'—says it all.

- It is called the man's curse, but a brand is associated with that curse—the daily shave and Gillette. The company's first safety razor, using a disposable blade, came as early as 1902, and the product continued for thirty years. In 1934, Gillette introduced the new 'Twist to Open' (TTO) design, in which the razor head stayed within the handle and emerged only with a twist of the same. In 1958, the company introduced the first 'adjustable razor', in which the blade could be adjusted in proportion to the closeness of the shave. The product ran for another twenty-eight years, until 1986. Gillette kept up with the times as the way the daily shave occurred was changing; it was no longer a relaxed daily affair, the pressure of daily routines did not allow a man much time for the morning ritual—and yet nothing started off the day better than a close shave. To keep up with the changing times and mindsets, Gillette launched:

  - Techmatic: a single-blade razor with a disposable cartridge;
  - Trac II: the world's first two-blade razor debuting in 1971;
  - Good News: the first disposable double-blade razor in 1976;
  - Atra: debuted in 1977, with a pivoting head;
  - Gillette Sensor: debuted in 1990, with spring-loaded blades;
  - Sensor Excel: arrived in 1993, with a piece of

rubber at the bottom of the cartridge that helped raised facial hairs, aiding a better shave;

- Sensor 3: introduced three blades.
- Mach 3: debuted in 1998; Mach 3 Turbo came with ten strips, double the original;
- M3 Power was the battery-powered version of the Mach 3 Turbo;
- Gillette Fusion: a five-bladed razor appeared in 2006, with a sixth blade at the rear for precision trimming and beard shaping; Fusion Power was the motorized version of Gilette Fusion.
- Fusion Proglide and Proglide Power: these were launched in 2010.

From producing just a blade required for a shave, Gillette moved with the times to produce blades that have become a part of every man's daily chores—most people's knowledge of blades beyond Gillette is very little. Gillette is now part of Procter & Gamble, which is a power brand by itself and has many more stories to tell when it comes to long-term brand sustainability.

Brand Rajini Sustained Value Propositions

For the consumer who was watching films for 150 minutes of pure bliss, Brand Rajini was a safe bet. Brands fail when they forget to provide consistent value propositions to the consumer. In the decades of the 1980s and 1990s, Brand Rajini assured entertainment value. But that came through continuous value propositions that emanated from all Rajini films during that time. Brand Rajini ensured that the essential character of the entertainment never changed, that the expectations implanted in the minds of its consumers were never bent, and that it never followed any fads. Brand Rajini, which had firmly established its space in the southern part of the country, was now launched to the north of Vindhyas. Paired with his mentor and role model, Amitabh Bachchan, Rajini was first and foremost not dismissed in his new region of foray: he had a way of speaking Hindi that was accepted by audiences and his first movie, *Andha Kanoon*, was a blockbuster. *Gangvaa, John Jani Janardhan* and a host of Hindi action films were not trendsetters, but Rajini performed with gusto, attracting attention and delivering moderately successful movies, including *Chaalbaaz*, where he was noticed and appreciated for his role. Mukul Anand's *Hum*, released in early 1991, brought Rajini together with Amitabh Bachchan again. Despite a small role, Rajini captured the northern audience with his brand of humour and action, living up to the expectations of the audience.

Some global brands that have successfully sustained their value propositions can be seen below.

- Colonel Harland Sanders first served his fried chicken at a gas station in 1930 and became so successful that in 1935 he was titled the 'Kentucky Colonel', recognizing his contribution to the cuisine. His Sanders Court and Cafe generally served travellers, but when Interstate 75 was being built and it bypassed his location, he sold his property and began to sell his chicken to restaurant owners. Kentucky Fried Chicken (KFC) opened in 1952; by the 1960s, it was sold in over 600 outlets in the US. Sanders sold KFC in 1964 and it went through three owners until the present. The recipe of eleven herbs and spices used by KFC in preparation of its chicken remains a trade secret. KFC sells chicken in many varieties: fried, grilled, breasts, thighs, drumsticks, wings, kebabs, etc. It also serves sandwiches and burgers, pies and desserts, and has incorporated many local cuisine elements as in India. Today, when it comes to fast-food chicken, KFC always comes first because of the value it offers to its customers.

- Bayerische Motoren Werke AG, known to the world as BMW, came into being in 1917 after the restructuring of Rapp Motorenwerke, an aircraft engine manufacturing firm which was forced to cease production because of the Versailles Treaty. BMW commenced motorcycle production in 1923 and cars in 1928. Its first car was based on an Austin (UK) design and called the Dixi. There was no stopping BMW after this. It continued to produce automobiles with the driver in mind and came up with different product offerings for a range of customers; these have evolved over time as:

  - 3 series: a compact executive car released in 1975;
  - 5 series: a mid-sized executive car;

- 6 series: an executive coupe and convertible class;
- 7 series: a full-sized luxury vehicle;
- M series: M signifying motorsport, these are cars that have modified engines, transmissions and suspensions and target the sporty driver;
- 1 series: launched in 2004, a car targeting the compact family;
- SUV and SAV: BMW also produces sports utility vehicles as the X5 and sports activity vehicles as the X1, X3 and a mid-sized luxury crossover X6.

Brand Rajini Revelled in Its Heritage and Consistency

A distinguishing brand attribute that enables it to sustain its competitive advantage is its heritage. There is a famous saying by Thomas Edison: that genius is one per cent inspiration and ninety-nine per cent perspiration. Great brands have one common trait: they took time and worked hard to build a meaningful and relevant past—their heritage. So it was with Brand Rajini. The story of Brand Rajini by the 1990s was crisp, meaningful, relevant and memorable.

Heritage is about living in the minds and hearts; when a product or personality secures that place, it becomes a brand. Brand Rajini's heritage was always kept transparent. The bus conductor, the penniless youth who sought training with a friend's support, the wanderings in the film world in search of a role, the steadfast respect for his mentor, the slow and steady building of his fame and reputation, the modesty in success, the declaration and acceptance of failures—everything about Brand Rajini was about its heritage.

- In 1893, a journalist, social reformer and freedom fighter, Nageshwara Rao Pantulu, established a patent medicine business in Mumbai and shifted operations to Chennai in 1914. You feel pain, and then it is gone—this was the mantra on which Amrutanjan was centred. It is the quintessential pain-relief balm, and there is no better substitute. The bottle still recalls its heritage with the word Bombay inscribed on its lid. The yellow-coloured balm in the little glass bottle is a part of almost every Indian household, particularly prominent in the South India. At the same time, Amrutanjan has transformed itself into an ever-young product with new packaging and variants. There are three key variants now: a pain-relief balm, a strong balm and a maha-strong balm. Plus, the brand has extended into segments such as roll-on analgesic, cold-gel packs, reusable gels, joint-ache creams and sprays in the quest for new users. As the brand made the transformation from regional to national, it retained one attribute—its grip over rural and semi-urban markets. That has been the heart of Amrutanjan's distribution strategy—keeping its key consumer profile intact even as it seeks new users. Amrutanjan is now so much a part of the Indian lifestyle that sometimes people reportedly apply the balm before retiring for the night—just for old times' sake!

- In 1824, John Cadbury began selling tea, coffee and drinking chocolate, which he produced himself, at Bull Street in Birmingham, England. Chocolates were then only an indulgence of the wealthy. John Cadbury partnered with his brother Benjamin and the company they formed was called Cadbury Brothers of Birmingham. In 1854, the brothers got a Royal Warrant for producing chocolates for Queen Victoria. Soon they acquired an estate and christened it Bournville. In 1905, Cadbury launched its Dairy Milk bar, which became its bestselling product by 1913. Fruit and Nut (1928), Whole Nut (1933), Flake (1920), Cream-filled Eggs (1923), Crunchie (1929) and Roses (1938) are all part of Cadbury's heritage, and they fill the shelves even today. Cadbury India began its operations in India in 1948 by importing chocolates. It now has manufacturing facilities in Thane, Induri (Pune) and Malanpur (Gwalior), Bangalore and Baddi (Himachal Pradesh) with a market share of over seventy per cent and is on the list of the 100 topmost trusted brands. A simple birthday gift, an expression of love, a sense of fulfilment, a simple mouthful of relish or just nostalgia—Cadbury is part of everyone's heritage.

Brand Rajini Promoted Fellowship, Not Brand Wars

When you compete with other brands, the game can become deadly. Brands beget warfare. And brand vocabulary includes terms such as feud, guerrilla marketing and target shoot-outs. The famous brand wars began with the cola wars, Coke versus Pepsi. Thereafter, we saw Microsoft versus Apple, and now there is Facebook versus Google. Consumers also formed their own affiliations, which resulted in India's very own Scorpio versus Safari, Maruti versus Hyundai and Airtel versus Vodafone wars. The wars between competing brands in the same space are legendary. But Brand Rajini differentiated in this aspect. It was clear by the mid 1980s that the next legends in the Tamil film industry were Rajinikanth and Kamal Haasan. History was about to repeat its act, when fans were divided between MGR and Sivaji Ganesan. Brand Rajini took a different path—in fact, it created a distinct and separate path in order to never invade or poach in the other's territory and thus create a divide.

Rajini and Kamal were known to be the best of friends. They always complemented one another and appreciated each other's success. Brand Rajini openly declared that it was Kamal who suggested that each of them create a distinct path of his own.

From the 1980s, fans of the industry lost out watching the two emerging icons on the same screen. At the same time, Rajini soon became well-known for giving to others equal opportunities, big roles and work in films that were not centred on him. Rajini never forgot his mentor, acting in many movies produced by him. The same applied to many who initially took the risk to put him on a pedestal.

Brand Rajini epitomized fellowship, camaraderie, amity, gratitude and friendship with everyone in the industry. Fellowship in turn promoted customer attraction for Brand Rajini. By welcoming healthy competition, Brand Rajini transformed itself from a power brand to a darling brand.

Compare this with the way in which one of the world's biggest brands has conducted itself.

- How does one city capture the essence of everything you need in life? Why do the best of the best in the world work from this city? Because it is a fellowship city—New York. The city traces its roots to 1624, when it was founded as a trading post by colonists of the Dutch Republic. The city and its surroundings came under English control in 1664 and was christened New York after King Charles II of England granted the lands to his brother, the Duke of York. New York served as the capital of the United States from 1785 until 1790, and has been the country's largest city since then. And today New York is considered the cultural capital of the world.

  - It is a prominent location for the American entertainment industry.
  - It hosts thirty-nine large theatres (with more than 500 seats each), collectively known as Broadway, the theatre district.
  - It is a centre for the television, advertising, music, newspaper and book publishing industries, and is also the largest media market in North America.
  - Seven of the world's top eight global advertising

agency networks have their headquarters in New York.

- Two of the 'Big Four' record labels' headquarters are in New York City (Sony Music Entertainment and Warner Music Group).
- More than 200 newspapers and 350 consumer magazines have an office in the city.
- The television industry developed in New York and is a significant employer in the city's economy.
- New York City's food culture includes a variety of world cuisines influenced by the city's immigrant history and population. New York is a global hub of international business and is one of three 'command centres' for world economy (along with London and Tokyo).
- The New York Stock Exchange on Wall Street is the world's largest stock exchange by total market capitalization of its listed companies.
- New York City's population is exceptionally diverse.

All of these speak of the city's culture of encouraging fellowship amidst its inhabitants and industries. If any of these were to not allow another in the same category to co-exist, the city would have suffered and not been one of the foremost destinations in the world, whether for business or leisure. New York, one can see if one studies the city's history and culture in depth, is all about fellowship.

Brand Rajini: The Making of a Power Brand—Takeaways

Don't alienate your customers	Choose a path, positioning and strategy, and execute. Do your homework and then focus on execution. Don't get caught up in fads, thereby alienating your customers and making them shift to other brands. Brand Rajini continued to win more customers rather than distancing them.
Don't offer too much	Offer product values or services that are your core strengths and which customers want from you, else customers will lose interest. Brand Rajini ensured that it remained within the boundaries of wholesome entertainment.
Expand your limits within brand perception	Offering too much versus expanding limits should be carefully weighed. Brands have to expand but at the same time not steer away from their main course.
Focus on brand values	The value proposition should always be forthcoming. Brands have to stand by their values and not be shaken by market demands.
Be transparent; show integrity	Brand integrity should never be lost. Customers will lose faith as soon as the brand is not transparent. Brand Rajini was all about transparency and integrity.
Brands are bigger than products	Despite all the siblings a brand creates and the brand extensions it innovates, a brand should realize that it is bigger than the products it serves up. Brand Rajini was not about the films, it was about itself.

Remember your heritage	A brand's heritage is its strongest virtue. Don't hide it away, harp on it—after all, a brand does not become so without effort.

5

Brand Rajini: A Super Brand and an Icon

As brands reach the summit of the power brand status, their sustainability relationships with their customers need to be looked at differently. Brands are no longer the sum of their products—they don't belong to the company but to the people. Power brands have already garnered presence, visibility and customer satisfaction. To enhance further, the effort has to be on bonding emotionally with people in their day-to-day lives, kindling their passion and attraction, and maintaining that deep relationship. The brand's target objectives become even more complex as it begins to delve into the vagaries of a customer's emotions. Marc Gobe, in his book *Emotional Branding: The New Paradigm for Connecting Brands to People*, says that emotional branding focuses on 'the most compelling aspect of the human character: the desire to transcend material satisfaction and experience emotional fulfilment.' Gobe posits that brands are uniquely situated to accomplish this because they 'can tap into the aspirational drives which underlie human motivation.'

- Some associate this nine-letter name with a snob and critics proclaim that its snowflake logo is 'bird splat', but—ask a connoisseur, the professional who wants his image complete, the window-shopper who yearns for it when he sees it in an exclusive showroom or simply the jealous man whose eyes catch that snowflake peeping out of someone else's pocket—for its consumers, it's an aspirational bond with the brand: Mont Blanc. When choice transcends functional benefits, when you feel that you have reached somewhere in your life, when you want to gift yourself something to reflect the milestones you have achieved, Mont Blanc is your authoritative lifestyle trendsetter. The Meisterstuck name for its cornerstone model translates to 'masterpiece'; the white, stylized six-point star logo with round edges representing the snow-capped mountain was adopted in 1913. Today, the Mont Blanc brand is a lifestyle brand extending to watches, wallets, sunglasses and leather accessories.

- No one can miss its classic smell, the prickling when applied on an injured knee, the amber gold colour and the 'clouding' effect in water that recalls childhood memories, the green and white packaging that reminds one of the hospital, the sword on the label that conveys its 'protector' status—Dettol has been the quintessential 'cuts and wounds' brand from the 1930s. It is now perceived as the 'protector from germs' by consumers. Dettol's consumers feel safe, secure from germs and protected against viruses, owing to the deep connection that they have had with the brand for many years. The brand's tagline, 'Be 100% Sure', is all about the trust and the emotional bond built with its customers.

- One of the most enduring brands that has been associated with babies from as early as 1893 is the 'baby company' Johnson & Johnson, which started with surgical dressing products in the 1880s. Creating a talcum powder that removed the irritation resulting from plaster, the brand found that the product was so soothing that it became a remedy for diaper rash—soon, the baby powder with its distinctive smell found its way into every home. Despite many brands that have attempted to compete, no mom or dad ordinarily prefers to think of a brand of baby products other than Johnson's for their child. In fact, the product is so entrenched in consumer minds that today it is sometimes difficult to distinguish the smell of a baby from the smell of Johnson's Baby Powder. Despite a host of other popular brands emerging from the company's stable, which have created their own niche (Band-Aid, for instance), to everyone, Johnson & Johnson will always remain the 'baby company'— such is the power of its emotional connect.

- Mothers and doctors like and recommend alike the Hamam the family bath soap—built around this statement, the earlier Hamam advertisements showed a mother explaining the meaning of trust to her child using the example of Hamam. A doctor's-favourite prescription brand for minor skin allergies, it has for over eighty years been steadfast in its consumers' minds, fighting competition and changing environments. Hamam as a family soap is reflected in its three variants, the 'sampoorna snaan', Hamam 'scrub bath' and 'abhyanga snaan'. Hamam is a perfect embodiment of a deep-rooted emotional relationship between a brand and its customers.

Power brands focus on customer connectivity and intimacy, which does not come easily. A power brand has to not only retain customers, inducing them to make repeat purchases, but also create a ritual so that it starts to invade their lives and becomes part of it. Power brands transform their customers—they become the brands' cheerleaders. As Marc Gobe says, 'The biggest misconception in branding strategies is the belief that branding is about "market share" when it is really always about "mind and emotions share."'

The Emotional Branding of 'Brand Rajini': The Birth of a Superstar

The decade of the nineties saw the surge of liberalization, and a world of opportunities opened up for India, which was fiercely forging forward as the IT-service capital of the world. India started celebrating its young population. Newfound opportunities upgraded living standards. The growth of technology seeped into the daily living of the upmarket and urban Indian, who now sought changes in the entertainment industry. The celluloid world saw the demise of 'the angry young man', the feel-good factor established itself in movie themes, and families sought wholesome entertainment outside their living rooms. Malls and multiplexes changed the way people went to watch films. Going to a film became akin to a picnic. The picnic was becoming expensive and consumers wanted 'paisa vasool' or full value for money. The outcome was the local audience lapping up a spate of Hollywood's most extravagant offerings: *Terminator 2, Jurassic Park, Independence Day, The Lion King, Men in Black* and even the intensely gripping *Saving Private Ryan*. And Bollywood's emerging Khan trio started invading the areas south of the Vindhyas with their boisterous fare. How would the local Brand Rajini keep up with this competitive sweepstakes and emerge victorious?

Rajini forged ahead by building a bond with customers' emotions that went beyond loyalty. Rajini created a fan base that claimed 'I am with you, no matter what'. Rajini energized communications with a new found 'punch', his films changed from qualitative to preferential, enhancing their viewing to a unique experience. Rajini also went through upheavals, in an industry-shaking event, as we will see in the following pages, where he resurrected himself by replacing honesty with trust and transforming dishonour into love. Simply put, Rajini built such a relationship with his audience that it even made educated and smart people act in a less than rational manner—a Rajini fan became a Rajini fanatic. This time too, it was not easy; it came out of a stupendous effort—his 'navaratnas' ('nine gems') beginning from 1991.

- *Thalapathi*, 1991
- *Mannan*, 1992
- *Annamalai*, 1992
- *Veera*, 1994
- *Baashha*, 1995
- *Muthu*, 1995
- *Arunachalam*,1996
- *Padayappa*, 1999
- *Chandramukhi*, 2002

From Rajini Films to the Rajini Experience

India's best-known contemporary director Mani Ratnam (whose *Nayagan* figures in the 2005 *Time* magazine's best 'All-Time 100 Movies' list) launched *Thalapathi* ('Commander'), bringing together two giants of the film industry, Rajinikanth and Mammootty. The film set high expectations. Rajini appeared at its launch function with a sword in hand—the sign of a commander. *Thalapathi* presented a modern version of the tale of two best friends from Indian mythology, the friendship between Karna and Duryodhana in the Mahabharata. Rajini took on the role based on Karna—a character remembered by all Indians for his loyalty and philanthropy. The Rajini experience begins from his introductory shot. The voice of the mother yearning for her long-lost son fades away, and in full panoramic view, occupying the entire screen, enters a violent Rajini, ready to attack, against the backdrop of rain lashing down at a dhobi-ghaat. The audience gasped and got goose-flesh, signalling that there was no stopping Rajini hereafter—both in the film and in the making of a superstar. The opening fight sequence concluded to 'Rakkamma kaiya thattu' (Rakkamma, clap your hands'), a song which figures in one of BBC's lists of top ten songs in the world. Every scene, till the very end, when Rajini avenges the killing of his dear friend with the dialogue 'Yenna nee en nanban' (Because you are my friend') remained etched in memory. Everyone left the hall with an emotional Rajini experience—fans could ask for no more. For the new breed of Rajini connoisseurs, *Thalapathi* was the trailblazer of the Rajini experience. There was more to come. In *Thalapathi*, Brand Rajini learnt its first lesson of a being superstar—its brand of films not only had to fulfil people's needs (to go for a good, well-conceived film) but also their desires (to come out drenched with a Rajini experience). As Marc Gobe says in his book, 'Products fulfil needs, experiences fulfil desires.'

Consider the following example.

- When someone buys this brand, it represents change and evolution within the person, giving them a sense of achievement, a feeling of self-worth—when you say Mercedes, there is an immediate association with luxury, class and style. A person driving a Merc symbolizes the entrance into a completely different level of culture and affluence. No car company exemplifies the concept of innovation and transformation like Mercedes-Benz. Simply put, the brand transforms the person who owns it. From the creators of the first petrol-powered car, every Merc is recognized by its three-pointed star, symbolizing its ambition of universal motorization—it is a star that guides motorists everywhere. And it is a brand that changes life and experience for the person who owns the product.

From Fans to People

Fans and fanatics have their own unique way of showcasing their love for their hero. Brand Rajini, as a power brand, had to expand its customer base and make all consumers rejoice with the same experience as its fan base.

As the decade of the 1990s began, consumers across the nation—in fact, the world—got demarcated into age groups. There were the forty-niners and above (also referred to as 'the baby boomers'), the twenty-niners and above ('Gen X') and the youngest lot ('Gen Y'). The baby boomers predominantly held positions of authority and power; for them, life revolved around success, standing and accomplishment. Gen X comprised the young, well-educated, inspired and inventive group of people in their early thirties, whose focus was on vision, inspiration and relationships. And, finally, Gen Y consisted of the younger bunch of people who were looking for pure fun, interaction and instant gratification. How could all of this be packaged into a 150-minute screenplay, loaded with songs, action, dialogue and dramatic scenes, apart from a good story?

Using a brilliant rapport with a set of creators specializing in screenplay, dialogue writing, music and direction, Rajini carefully orchestrated the bringing together of the three segments' attractions. In fact, Rajini brought them all together as one family unit.

Sample this:

- *Annamalai* (1992): In one clean sweep, *Annamalai* grabbed hold of the entire family for gratification in parts and an experience as a whole. The creators perhaps envisioned it just right and christened Rajini 'Superstar Rajini' in the opening credits, to give a feel on the upcoming Rajini experience. *Annamalai* provided a complete Rajini package for the family with:

  - The lover saying 'Kadavule, Kaduvale' ('Oh God, Oh God') when he sees what he is not supposed to see and the anguish and anger at his friend's betrayal; the thumping of his thigh; his roar ('Malai da, Annamalai') and the swift walk of confidence; his self-starter approach to become a successful entrepreneur: to capture Gen X;
  - The fun-and-frolic slapstick with the snake: for Gen Y;

- ◆ The elderly gentleman who does not forget his past, his upbringing and his heritage: for the baby boomers.

With *Annamalai*, Rajini also reaffirmed his fan base amidst the female cine-going audience.

- *Mannan* (1992): This was a film that captured the heart of Gen X as they remembered every encounter of Rajini, the simple but self-righteous man married to an arrogant and rich wife. The entire audience identified emotionally when he sang 'Ammavendru azhaigatha' ('There is no living soul who doesn't utter the word mother'). The style he exhibited in the scene where he protects the ego of his arrogant wife at an elite gathering by dressing up like a gentleman and narrating what culture is all about to the crowd, lighting his cigarette at the end in his classic style, floored Gen X as well as Gen Y and brought smiles to the faces of the ageing baby boomers.

- *Muthu*: (1995):

  - ◆ The movie even captured audiences across the shores in Japan, the land of Akira Kurosawa (the film maker who inspired many a Hollywood film), and the media called this movie a 'haiku for Rajini'; Rajini became the 'Dancing Maharaja': never a good dancer, Rajini demonstrated the power of a super brand—the perception it creates in the eyes of the consumer; Japanese bars would play 'Thillana Thillana';

♦ Filled with an undertone of political satire, Rajini induced people to believe that a career in politics might lie ahead with his opening dialogue: 'Naan naan yeppo varuvaen, eppadi varuvaennu yaarukum thriyathu, aana vara vendia nerathilla correcta varuvaen' ('No one knows when and how I will come, but I will always appear at the right time')—words cannot describe the rapture of the audience at these words as whistles and shouts filled the theatre; that he could make an entire family whistle and shout together was a mark of Rajini's power;

♦ Prime Minister Manmohan Singh mentioned the success of the movie in his speech at DIET in 1996;

♦ The Japanese tourist when visiting Chennai now had a new agenda—seeing Rajinikanth, the comedian Senthil and the actress Meena.

Power brands have to attract people of all segments. There has to be something in it for everyone—that is perhaps what distinguishes a super brand from a power brand. And Brand Rajini was now a super brand.

One can see a similar all-segments-capture executed by another global brand.

• Meaning 'Little nest' in Swiss, Nestle was started in 1867 by Henri Nestle, who was searching for a healthy, economical and easy-to-use alternative to breastfeeding for mothers. Nestle was a pharmacist by profession who targeted infants as his customer base. Nestle branding was about creating and sustaining a brand for the entire family, and its eight product lines showcased the branding strategy that targets specific needs of customer segments. It had bottled water (Nestle Pure Life), infant formula (Lactogen), breakfast cereal (Nestle Cornflakes and Kokocrunch), baby food (Cerelac), milk products (NIDO, Nestle Cream, etc.), beverages (Nescafe), chocolates and confectionary (KitKat) and finally food (Maggi noodles). Each segment had a power brand and the word Nestle was attached to each brand—it was a super brand that catered to an entire family. It is perhaps no wonder that in 2011 Nestle was listed as number one in the Fortune Global 500 list as the world's most profitable corporation. It operates in eighty-six countries, with over 450 factories, and is still growing.

Quality to First Choice

Without a quality product, there is no brand. That quality has to come at the right price and the customer has to derive value. These are fundamentals—but what will make that brand a first choice? As you walk in the mall looking for jeans, you see many of the popular brands (e.g., Levis, Wrangler, Lee, Zara), including the one which is your favourite, but what is your first choice?

There is that intangible preference that comes from your emotions, your desire that goes beyond the quality of the product. This is true for films too, and Brand Rajini had to posit that attraction for customers. Although Rajini had the experience, in the way that quality films were brought out from his stable, it was time to make those films the first choice of the customer. Rajini's films had to have that extra tinge of emotional connect, some amount of redefinition of his heroism, a tweak in his usual styles, and perhaps some redefinitions of a Rajini experience. Rajini came up trumps with this branding strategy in his magnum opus *Baashha* and an equally exciting roller-coaster ride in *Padayappa*.

- *Baashha* (1995): *Baashha* is often cited as the film that catapulted Rajini to the stratosphere of superstardom in the Indian film industry. Rajini came out with a modification to his image as an action king—a hero can be beaten by the goons, but not his courage, valour, bravery, boldness and gallantry. *Baashha* was, in this sense, a masterpiece. The conversion of Manikkam the auto driver into Manik Baashha the don; the way Baasha walks; his bearing from start to finish; the intelligence he exhibits each time when dealing with Anthony the villain; and the grand finale of it all, the everlasting, powerful dialogue: 'Naan oru thadava sonna nooru thadavai sonna mathiri' ('If I say it once, it means I have said it a hundred times')—provided a completely new and enriching Rajini experience. Akin to cricket fans, Rajini fans watched the film in groups—it was if the thrill of the test match, the one-day match and the twenty-twenty match had combined together in 150 minutes of pure enjoyment. For the baby boomer, fulfilment came in the scene where Rajini gets the medical college seat and the simple answer he gives his sister on how he got it: 'Unmaya sonnenmaa' ('I told the truth'). Gen X and Gen Y were hooked by Baashha's successful walk with his team in tow, in tune to the movie's theme music, and his punch dialogue. There is only one Sachin for class, but for the mass there was only one Rajini. In fact, with *Baashha*, he made the word 'mass' into a new acronym—Most Admired Super Star!

- *Padayappa* (1997): 'En vazhi thani vazhi' ('My way is a unique way') was the hallmark punchline of Superstar Rajini in this roller-coaster ride of a film. *Padayappa* was another outstanding example of brand fellowship; Rajini gave an equally important and powerful role to the actress Ramya Krishnan—it was similar to a Borg-McEnroe final, a Gavaskar-Lillee tussle or a Sachin-Warne war in the sporting arena. *Padayappa*, in one way, stands testimony to Rajini's life itself—his dialogue which translates to 'You don't get something without real effort; what you get without effort does not stay with you for long'—it gave gratification to the baby boomers and a sent great message to Gen X and Gen Y.

Brand Rajini's awareness and presence had been achieved already, but with the completion of *Padayappa* Rajini was loved by all. His character and charisma made his personality special. The experience with his brand of films was more than visuals; it forged a permanent emotional connection with one and all. *Baashha* and *Padayappa* did something unique when it came to Rajini's films: if people went for a recent release or a current hit and found a full house, they didn't want to return disappointed; and there would always be the inducement to see it again because they wanted their 'picnic' experience completed and repeated. That is the hallmark of a super brand—it is not only your first choice but also your best choice and your repeated choice.

- What is the first choice for a global customer to order something off the web, or simply check the price of a book, a DVD, an electronic good or a fashion accessory? It is Amazon.com. Amazon describes its vision of business as 'relentlessly [focusing] on customer experience by offering [its] customers low prices, convenience and a wide selection of merchandise.' The founder Jeff Bezos's vision was to create the 'earth's biggest store'. Amazon's core business focuses on gaining repeat purchases by providing users functionality, fast and reliable fulfilment, timely customer service, feature-rich content and, most importantly, a trustworthy and secure transaction environment. Feature-rich content of product reviews, wish-lists and recommendations are created by Amazon for its customers, giving them the lowest price for the most popular product. Amazon is also a technology company which deeply integrates into its operations high-performance transaction systems, workflow and queuing systems, business intelligence and data analytics, neural networks and probabilistic decision-making. With the surge in e-books and their popularity, Amazon launched its proprietary e-reader, Kindle, which has now developed into a full-fledged tablet gadget. And the purchase of a Kindle convinces customers to repeatedly revisit and reorder from Amazon by streamlining and smoothening the retail process even further.

The Brand Rajini 'Punch' Mantra

Brand communication creates a direct relationship between the brand and its consumer. The objectives are met when the message is in line with the recipient's existing convictions and outlook. Brands and products typically use a 'brand champion' or a 'brand ambassador' to facilitate this. It may be the company's CEO or a well-established icon—a sportsperson or a film star with whom the audience can quickly and easily relate. The brand champion is the key storyteller for the brand and this story has to be repeatedly communicated in different forms. The brand's message should embody the three important characteristics of good brand communiqués:

- Clarity: an authentic and strong brand message;

- Consistency: the way the same message is sent through different media channels;

- Constancy: the art of having these messages remembered by the consumers.

Rajini converted key dialogues in his film to punchlines for himself. It was Brand Rajini's way of enhancing the communication. Fans, and the audience in general, received these messages as they related to them. As co-author P. C. Balasubramanian says in his introduction to *Rajini's Punchtantra: Business and Life Management the Rajinikanth Way*, 'From a coolie to a CEO, from a small-time entrepreneur to a big businessman, from an urchin to a postgraduate, from a maid to an activist, from lovers to siblings, from spouses to in-laws—I have seen "Rajini dialogues" evoke deep resonance in all, often accompanied by a sparkle in the eye, a nod of acceptance and a smile of acknowledgement. The statements have touched them and remained deep within.' Perhaps *Baashha* truly emphasized the concept of Rajini's 'punch'; besides the famous *Baashha* punchline quoted earlier, it also personified Rajini's punch with:

- 'Pon, penn, pugazh pinnadi ambalai poga koodathu, ambalainga pinnala ithellaam varanum' ('Don't chase wealth, woman and fame; these should follow you');

- 'Nallavanga aandavan sodhipaan, kaivida maatan... kettavangalukku aandavan neraya kudupaan, aana kai vittuduvaan' ('God tests good people but does not let them down...He may give the bad ones generously but lets them down');

- 'Namma vaazhkai namma kailathaan irrukku' ('Our life is in our hands');

- 'Vaazhkaila bayam irrukalam, aana bayamae vazhkai ayuda koodathu' ('It is fine to fear some things in our life, but fear itself should not rule our life');

- 'Naama nammala gavanichhaathan aandavan nammala gavanippaan' ('Only when we take care of ourselves will God take care of us').

With these, Rajini's punchlines became a key factor in his films, adding to his style and substance of dialogue delivery. Brand Rajini used it as a means of directly communicating lines that were close enough to match the audience's beliefs and ideologies.

- These are not the brand's taglines—they are simple statements of truth and they are always current. A bit of humour, a tinge of a pun, as told by a little boy and girl—Amul's communiqués to its consumers were always 'utterly and butterly.' You always see Amul Butter as the face-saver in the situation. An assortment of Amul Butter advertising billboards, comprising catchphrases that came with equally well-drawn cartoons:

- 'Out of the world on any dish' (on the invasion of satellite channels);
- 'Do buttered pilots need more bread? Amul, don't stir, just spread' (on pilots' stir for increase in payscales);
- 'Will abolishing octroi stop greasing palms? Amul ka maska lagao' (on the octroi toll controversy);
- 'Speak less, eat more. Munching Time No Limit' (when MTNL raised local call rates);
- 'Utterly butter*lie* detector. Amul, truly the best' (on the use of lie detectors during the stock market scam investigation);
- 'Dollar becomes taller, Amul makes cents always' (on the falling rupee);
- 'Please fasten your eat belts! Amul, King of Food Times' (on the financial crisis of Kingfisher airlines);
- 'Kuchh raaz...kuchh naraaz. Amul, 2Gud to resist' (on the 2G scam);
- 'www.faceblock.com... Amul, post on toast' (on the central minister's idea of screening social media);
- 'Yeh Bugtameez kaun hai? Amul, undercover, overbread' (on the bugging of the finance minister's office);
- 'Forget Scamul, enjoy Amul' (farewell to 2010, the year of scams).

Each of Amul's statements were close to the feelings, emotions and beliefs of the common Indian man on issues facing the country or the world—and it enabled him to remember Amul at all times.

Honesty to Truth: Brand Rajini Fails and Resurrects

We live in an era where product sales are induced more by customer emotions than marketing efforts. When the product fails, the brand—and not the product—takes the entire blame. As Matt Haig says in his book *Brand Failures*, 'emotions aren't to be messed with. Once a brand has created that necessary bond [with customers], it has to handle it with care. One step out of line and the customer may not be willing to forgive.' Haig goes on to state some of the crucial reasons for brand failures:

- when a brand forgets what it is supposed to stand for;

- when a brand develops a tendency to overestimate its importance and its own capability;

- when a brand thinks it can take on the entire world by getting into every product category imaginable;

- when a brand tries to deceive the customer;

- when a brand loses its relevance, fails to kindle consumer passion and is out of sync with current traditions, belief and customs.

Brand Rajini had everything going for *Baba* (2002). It had as director Suresh Krishna, who had delivered three consecutive blockbusters, including *Baashha*; it had music by A. R. Rahman; and, armed with the best technicians and actors, it generated some of the best pre-release hype. Hidden somewhere in this excitement was another fact: Brand Rajini had extended an arm, taking responsibility for the film's production, story and screenplay. A film can have a great story, great actors performing stellar roles, soul-searching dialogue, lilting music, pleasing cinematography and high-cost production values, but its essence is in the screenplay. What the audience will see on the screen during the running time of the film will make or break its success. Why Rajini adopted that responsibility, going out of his core competence, will remain a mystery, but it brought him bad tidings.

A spate of events took place before and around the actual release: a local political party objected to certain lyrics in one of the songs and it had to be partially deleted; the party's leader spread propaganda that Rajini set a bad example for the youth in his role in *Baba*; intruders snatched a print using armed force; the moving spirit behind the film and Rajini's spiritual guru, Swami Sachidananda, passed away four days after the film's release. Things went further awry after the film's release on Independence Day: by the second day, the crowds dwindled, as word spread everywhere that it was a 'swami padam' ('godly movie') from Rajini. There were no reservations and theatres brooded over unsold tickets—a completely dismal and unexpected scenario for a Rajini film. By the fourth day, ticket prices were slashed—and still there was no improvement. By the end of the week, some exasperated distributors sought to meet Rajini to explain their losses and woes.

Brand failures all have the same pattern: a brand-shaking event, then a market reaction, and then a follow-up by the troubled brand—this last may put it on the road to recovery and even return it to its old glory, or it may result in a downward slide to a dusty death. The film business can also be termed a dirty business. In that murky world, nobody saves anybody else from a failed business transaction; at best, a successful actor will do another movie for the losing producer in the hope that it will succeed and balance the accounts.

Brand Rajini differed from the norms in the face of this failure. Much like the differentiation in histrionics, Brand Rajini made an unprecedented move in the industry by personally repaying the producers and distributors who suffered losses for *Baba*. It was a hallmark event in the industry that no one else would dare undertake. With that single stroke that spoke of accepting the truth of failure, taking responsibility for the disaster and financially recouping the lost monies, Brand Rajini won the hearts of many. He turned dishonour into love. The dent in Brand Rajini's make-up was repaired instantly and the wounds healed. But perhaps it was time to take stock. Predictions that *Baba* was the last of Rajini spread like wildfire. His following sabbatical for almost three years compounded the rumours. The brand had to resurrect itself. This fall was more intense than the first which came in the initial years. Would Rajini win the war of dharma now?

Super brands never give up. Failures are their stepping stones for further success. They bank on inherent strengths, their strong leadership, their staying relevant for their consumers, their passion to keep improving and emerging distinct from their competitors.

Rajini carefully launched his next film, *Chandramukhi,* in 2005. At the music album launch, Rajini stated with a clap of his hands: 'Naan yaanai illai, kuthirai, keezha vizhundha takkunu yezhunthupaen' ('I am not an elephant but a horse, for I get up instantly when I fall'). After almost ten years of stupendous success in Tamil cinema, Rajini chose a title that relied primarily on a female character—that itself was a huge change and a big gamble. The movie had a heroine-dominated story— no punchlines or political satire, and Rajini underplayed. While the movie retained the time-tested cocktail of Rajini humour, action and emotions, horror was also added as a new ingredient. Despite being a remake and a heroine-dominated movie, the last few minutes was engulfed by Rajini's acting histrionics: the descent from the stairs in a king's costume, along with fearsome-looking dogs held together by the king as he walked down, sent tremors through the audience, and the very popular 'Laka laka laka' scene enhanced the depth of the short act by Rajini.

Brand Rajini was resurrected, and the movie ran for over 800 days. Rajini's fans went into a frenzy and cried—they were overjoyed to see their hero back with a vengeance and, with verve and vigour, attain victory.

Brand Rajini took revenge for his previous failure through this stupendous success.

- In 2003, the Centre for Science and Environment (CSE) declared that aerated beverages produced by soft-drinks manufacturers, including multinational giants Coca-Cola and Pepsico, contained toxins including lindane, DDT, malathion and chlorpyrifos—pesticides that can cause a breakdown of the immune system. The CSE found that Pepsi's soft drink bottled in India had thirty-six times the level of pesticide residues permitted under EU regulations, whilst Coca-Cola had thirty times the allowable level; the CSE also said that it had tested the same products manufactured in the US and found no pesticides. This was disaster for the world's number one brand-equity holder, Coca-Cola. In 2004, an Indian parliamentary committee backed up the CSE's findings and a government-appointed committee was entrusted with developing the world's first pesticide standards for soft drinks. Coca-Cola India registered an eleven per cent drop in sales after the pesticide allegations. How did Coca-Cola come out of this rut? The mandatory press announcements, full-page advertisements and Q&As were released to ease the tension. But on a larger scale, Coca-Cola began its corporate social responsibility (CSR) undertakings to rebuff critics who were opposed to the advent of multinational companies (MNC) operating on Indian soil. Coca-Cola's CSR initiatives were not a one-time remedy but a continuous process. These included providing direct and indirect employment in its bottling plants, employing people who are disabled, implementing water conservation projects for better life for children, including rain-water harvesting. Through its continuous CSR initiatives in rural India, Coca-Cola intends to not just prevent dents in its brand value but also remain a brand leader in the beverages industry in India.

Brand Rajini showcased how a super brand should resurrect from failure by taking responsibility, never giving up on its values, providing strong leadership, staying relevant, improving on its core strengths and building equity—and thereby, in this particular case, owning the distinct position held over three decades in the film industry.

Brand Rajini: The Super Brand—Takeaways

Provide a sense of belonging	A brand needs to involve the consumers. If it simply communicates, the consumer will forget; if it remains visible and present, the consumer may remember; but involve the consumer, and he will understand. Brand Rajini gave a sense of belonging to his fans. They came together, they enjoyed and brooded together.

Clear vision	A brand needs to focus on its core strengths. As it gets more popular, it needs to keep a check on the brand ego—for, one wrong move will end in a disaster. Brand Rajini failed when it deviated from its vision.
Evangelism	A super brand needs to have a special appeal for consumers. A brand can, with crusading zeal, work for a particular cause that will cause followers to get associated with it. At the same time, a brand has to balance the cause and the benefit it derives financially and serves socially.
Storytelling	A super brand should never lose its grip on its consumers. It requires continuous storytelling to hit the emotions, desires and beliefs of its consumers. Brand Rajini always had storytelling, which sustains a superstar status, at the core.
Selling to relationships	Super brands are not selling single products any more. Healthy relationships with consumers enable them to take the repeat-purchase decision. Super brands have to continuously seek new ways of maintaining relationships with their consumers.
Experience to ritual	Every move a super brand makes should be converted to a ritual that invokes a consumer's passion, enthusiasm and faith in the brand. Super brands should create a mystery about the change they are about to bring in order to form an emotional connect that will result in converting the transactional aspect of buying to an experiential one.

6

Rajini the Cult Brand

The Power of a Cult Brand and Cult Branding

Power brands are like magnets: they create a magnetic field of influence. The more power the brand has, the more customers are attracted, repeatedly choose it and a passionate bond is created. Slowly, the brand assembles different groups with varied interests within this field of influence. That group swears by the brand, talks and lives by it and holds a common belief about it. When this single-minded devotion emerging from its loyal followers becomes known to the world, the brand's cheerleaders become a cult.

'Cult' usually refers to a movement whose beliefs or practices are considered abnormal or bizarre. But the actual meaning does not have a negative tone; it is derived from the Latin word *cultus* or the French *culte,* meaning 'worship'. Consequently, according to *An*

Introduction to Cult Branding: The Truth behind Customer Loyalty, cult brands are 'a special class of magnetic brands that command super-high customer loyalty and almost evangelical customers or followers who are devoted to them.' The moment we read this, brand images that come into our minds are Harley-Davidson and Apple.

Are all power, super and iconic brands cult brands? Not necessarily. Even an iconic brand may not be a cult brand—there is a dividing line, and there is an ongoing debate on this issue between brand honchos and pundits. But, simply put, a cult brand is different from all other brands, as:

- Customers of a cult brand find a sense of belonging and consider it an honour to be part of that cult.

- The brand creator keeps evolving in a way that it keeps its followers in a mood of enthusiasm, excitement and obsession; it never intimidates them.

- Cult brands generate passion in their followers—for instance, frenzy at a new product launch from the brand.

- A cult brand cuts across geography, culture, religion and language; the cult has strange bedfellows with the same causes and beliefs—they need no introduction, the moment they find they belong to the cult they are together.

- No one can create a cult brand overnight; it comes out of years of effort and well-crafted strategies to attract and retain customer bonding.

- As much as the brand cannot be built overnight, no one can become part of the cult overnight; it takes time—the brand has to grow on the person, and there has to be the conviction that there is mutual rhapsody.

A cult brand has a tremendous amount of responsibility. In order to be relevant to the cult group, it should develop an ethos or philosophy and act within its boundaries. The brand has to create a benign cult. Everything the brand does—its service, public image, press statements, media interviews—will have a major effect on the cult and therefore should be within the realms of the brand's philosophy. That will ensure that its ardent followers embrace it as part of their own identity and tell the world how proud they are because they belong to that cult. The Apple iPod, iPhone and the iPad launched within the boundaries of the cult of the Mac, making all users feel proud, distinct and as if they were holders of a new identity.

- There were two small levers in this motorcycle that their owners used to talk about: a small one below the clutch near your left hand, and another small one above the gear lever near your right foot. The former rescued the owner from the daily struggle of kick-starting the bike (a knack which is learnt over time) and the latter helped him to stop the bike without shifting gears. You could hear its thump from a distance, it was all-black, and stories said that if you hopped off the bike on the highway, so steady was it on the road that it could travel a great distance even without the rider! Whether you like it or loathe it, it is a cult brand in India—the Royal Enfield Bullet. Started as a British brand in 1890, Enfield started assembling bikes in India from 1955. Now owned by the Eicher Group, it is the oldest motorcycle company in the world and is the longest production run model. It is the emerging cult brand of India, and has a Bullet club in almost every city, with communities, blogs, trip logs and forums that go in tandem with the product's tagline 'Leave home [with a Bullet]'. The Himalayan Odyssey occurs every year when Bullet owners assemble to navigate the tough terrains in Ladakh. An all-women's Bullet club, 'HopOnGurls Royal Enfield Woman Riders Club', has a vision of helping women unwind and have fun and a mission of making the number of female Bullet riders equal male the number of Bullet riders in five years. From the greenery of Punjab to the deserts of Rajasthan to the rice-fields of Tamil Nadu, people flaunt the Bullet or aspire for it, and they say in a single voice: 'Once you ride a bullet, you don't ride any other bike.'

The Cult of Brand Rajini

A grand extravaganza was about to pitchfork into frenzy as fans waited in the wee hours of the dawn to get inside theatres across India on 15 June 2007. At the same time, a few lucky ones were already hung-over from the excitement of the previous evening. This was happening at the Dante Cinema Hall in Palermo, Italy, as word spread from Norway, Holland and across Europe that 'The Boss' had arrived—Rajini, in and as *Sivaji*. It was the first Tamil film releasing across the US, Canada, Europe, Singapore, Malaysia, South Africa, Sri Lanka and Australia. The film opened to a full house across 750 screens globally; sixteen theatres screened the same film in Chennai; it occupied 303 screens across Tamil Nadu, 300 in Andhra Pradesh, twelve in North India, four in New Delhi and 145 screens across other countries. Every theatre was booked for two weeks, assuring profits for the film's producer AVM Studios, the oldest one in the country. Overtaking every other film from the subcontinent, *Sivaji* was the costliest film of India with an estimated ₹80 crore budget. No one dared take such risks then; but the makers of the film were confident given the kind of cult following Brand Rajini had. People's 'picnic' had begun. And if they felt disappointed with the full-house situation for the next two weeks, there was *Chandramukhi* playing next door, completing its 800-day run.

A film release could not get better than this. The sheer demonstration of Brand Rajini's cult power—invoking deep passion and desire amongst his fans and viewers, with activities ranging from erecting sky-high posters of the hero, pouring milk over it, throwing flowers or burning incense—seemed like madness to those who did not belong to that cult.

In *Sivaji*, Brand Rajini was paired with a dream team. With S. Shankar as its director, the film had music by A. R. Rahman, art by Thotta Tharani, photography by K. V. Anand, and came with a number of catch-points that mesmerized the audience:

- Art director Thotta Tharani showcased a Babylonian palace for a song and upped the scale with a complete acrylic and glass set for another hit song, making the audience gasp at the sheer size and glory;

- Rajini was given a fair look with computer-generated imagery;

- The well-known designer Manish Malhotra designed Rajini's wardrobe for the movie while the French hair-stylist Sandrin Veriar Seth designed two different hairstyles for the film and thirteen hairstyles for one of the songs;

- Rahman's blast with 'Thee Thee' ('Fire, Fire') was made into a complete visual treat—a trademark of Director Shankar;

- 'Ballelaikka'—the opening word of the song came from a Russian music instrument which intrigued the audience about its source but then went on to become a simple catchphrase;

- Brand Rajini donned the names of the two legends in Tamil cinema—Sivaji and MGR—in his two roles, provoking debate about whether it was intentional;

- The movie was devoid of the famous punchlines that were one of the USPs of a Rajini film; yet, one of the regular lines, 'Paera kaetavudane chumma athuruthilae' ('Don't you feel the instant tremor when you hear the name?'), when uttered by Rajini in his own inimitable style, transformed into a punchline.

For the 150,000 odd fan clubs and the millions who watched the flick, it was Rajini mania. The cult's thirst and yearning for Rajini—who showed himself once in two years, was never seen on any product advertisements or TV shows and rarely in media interviews—was being satisfied. Pathans who got free tickets sponsored by a non-profit organization in the Persian Gulf came out of the hall saying 'Rajini, kya aadmi hai woh!' ('Rajini, what a man!') despite not understanding a word of dialogue. For the die-hard Rajini fan, the clincher came from his one-liner: 'Panningathaan kootama varum, singham singalathaan varum' ('Only swine travel in droves, the lion comes alone'). As Mathew W. Ragas and Bolivar J. Bueno say in *The Power of Cult Branding*, 'Cult branders enjoy incredible loyalty because they work hard to connect with their customers at the very highest level

[...] They don't just offer great products and services, but they understand needs for social interaction, esteem and self-actualization. They make customers believe that your brand has no equal.' With *Sivaji*, the cult of Brand Rajini was complete.

Brand Rajini's Courage and Determination: The Embodiment of a Cult Brand

Director Shankar is well-known in the industry circles for being a classic film maker who works to a bound script, screenplay, scenario and story-board. In 2001, he announced the project *ROBO* with the legendary Kamal Haasan. It did not take off for various reasons. In 2007, Shankar announced the project again with the iconic Indian film star Shah Rukh Khan, who was not only the hero but also became its producer. A couple of months later, the project was called off again. The fate of Director Shankar's dream venture seemed dismal. In early January 2008, after a series of speculative rumours, the surprising news that Rajini would don the mantle of 'Robot' broke. The film was rechristened *Enthiran*.

Thus began the tweets, the posts, the likes and dislikes about Brand Rajini's adopting what had been rejected by two actors. The question that arose in the minds of Brand Rajini's followers was: was Rajini taking another risk? Would a script written for the likes of Kamal Haasan and Shah Rukh Khan work for Rajini? Would a technology spectacle sidetrack the Rajini experience? But the answers to these questions lay in the character of Brand Rajini—it is a cult brand. In *The Power of Cult Branding*, the authors say that 'Consumers embrace cult brands and are loyal to them because their creators pushed the limit, took significant risk, and produced new and different things. Consumers are tired of being bombarded with products and services that all look the same, feel the same and act the same. They want surprises.'

Director Shankar's woes did not end. Eros and Ayngaran International backed out of the project, citing failures arising out of the global financial crisis, and Sun Pictures took over the producer's mantle. The film's estimated budget was touching ₹162 crores—doubling the cost incurred for *Sivaji*, and an equivalent risk. But the director remained steadfast as he orchestrated another visionary team that included Aishwarya Rai, the Indian woman's icon; Mary E. Vogt, who designed costumes for *Inspector Gadget* and *Men in Black*; Yuen Woo Ping, the stunt co-ordinator; and Stan Wiston Studios, which was responsible for the animatronics in *Jurassic Park*—a first in Indian cinema.

Shooting commenced in September 2008, starting at Peru, then moving to the US, Brazil and India, and was completed on 7 July 2010. Director Shankar lived his dream. His faith in Brand Rajini's courage in donning the mantle of 'Robot' did not go in vain. Brand Rajini's sheer effort and determination to portray a robot was the trump card.

Shattering *Sivaji*'s initials, *Enthiran* launched on 1 October 2010, opening to 2,250 prints across approximately 3,000 screens worldwide. There were

1,400 screens in Tamil Nadu, 128 in Kerala and forty-five in Karnataka. And, for the first time, Rajini properly captured North India, with the release of the film across 1,000 screens, with 750 prints. The commercial statistics of the film's success were earth-shattering. What the reporters wrote about the film, the brand and the cult was more interesting. A compendium:

- *Hollywood Reporter*, USA (Lisa Tsering): 'Rajini is such a badass that Chuck Norris is afraid of him. So goes the Internet lore of a sixty-year-old South Indian screen icon so potent that fans build temples to him, women swoon, and men just shrug and give up. Filmgoers with a taste for the absurd will be richly rewarded.'

- *The Independent*, UK (Andrew Bincombe): 'This weekend, the sixty-one-year-old veteran of more than 150 films is earning even more money. The star's latest film, *Enthiran*—English title *The Robot*—opened to good reviews and huge, adoring crowds who queued overnight outside cinemas across the nation to watch the latest, high-adrenalin adventure. Inside, the audiences shouted and cheered at their hero's unlikely moves, while outside fireworks were set off and drums played.'

- Genevieve Koski from the AV Club stated: 'Before you go into *Enthiran*, hoping for a something like an IndianCrank, nothing but high-octane action featuring K'nex-style robots, be warned: it isn't that. It can be loosely defined as a science-fiction/action movie, yes, but it's also an Indian movie made for Indian audiences, which means it gives over a lot— and I mean a lot.'

- After a screening at the Mumbai International Film Festival, American film director Oliver Stone praised *Enthiran* for being very original.

- Likewise, Jon Landau, producer of *Avatar* (2009), termed Rajini as amazing after viewing the film's trailer.

- On 13 December 2010, the Internet Movie Database (IMDB) announced its top 205 films of the world, among which *Enthiran* occupied the thirty-ninth spot with a score of 7.4/10. It is also the only Tamil film to be featured in this list.

- And finally, Grady Hendrix, writing for the online magazine *Slate*, said, 'He is no mere actor—he is a force of nature. If tiger had sex with a tornado and their "tiger-nado" baby got married to an earthquake, their offspring would be known as Rajinikanth.'

To keep up with a global release perhaps, theatres commenced screening as early as 4:00 a.m. in India. And when the cult of Rajini saw his onscreen performance, his disciplined effort in depicting a precision-timed sweetheart robot and then a determined yet terrifying villain robot, they simply came out of the hall, thrilled and satisfied, and said to the next waiting lot, 'Happy Diwali, folks.'

- A legendary icon, the late Steve Jobs directed development of the iPhone in 2005. Jobs revealed the iPhone to the public on 9 January 2007 at the Macworld 2007 convention and the phone went on sale in June 2007, when thousands of customers lined up over two nights outside stores nationwide. The passionate reaction of the launch made the media christen the product the 'Jesus Phone'. The sales spread across the UK and Europe in November and in Australia in spring 2008. In July 2008, Jobs upgraded the iPhone with 3G compatibility. Critics viewed it as costly, but the iPhone 3G's craze spread across the globe. By 2010, almost seventy-four million units had rolled out to consumers, generating more than fifty per cent of the total profits that global cell phone sales generate. In October 2011, Apple launched the iPhone 4S, which sold over a million models in the first twenty-four hours, slated to be the biggest launch of any mobile phone in the world. Apple surpassed all competitors to become the largest mobile phone company in the world. Steve Jobs had already envisioned the iPhone cult with Apple's support of third-party applications written in Ajax for the phone. Apple shared revenue with the developers. The iTunes store, which sold these applications, had crossed ten billion downloads by

January 2011. Steve Jobs was a visionary—he created the cult of the Mac computer, and then went on to create another cult with his cell phone.

Brand Rajini's Seduction of the Cult

HUMILITY

Marketing guru Seth Godin says, 'The humble brand understands that it needs to re-earn attention, re-earn loyalty and reconnect with its audience as if every day is the first day.'

For Brand Rajini, humility is DNA. Acknowledged by one and all, one does not need to be a Rajini fan to speak of his humility. When NDTV crowned him 'Entertainer of the Decade', presenter Prannoy Roy did not introduce him as a superstar or harp on his superlative success in the entertainment industry; he introduced Rajini as 'the most humble person' he had ever known. To a question by him on how he managed to be so humble, Rajini responded saying that was because of God that he got all the love from the producers, directors and fans, and God had made him humble.

In his speech to celebrate Kamal Haasan's fiftieth year in filmdom, Rajini openly stated how Kamal had helped him to branch out into his own terrain. He presented a perfect analogy of how the goddess of arts had kept Kamal at her hip (while keeping all the rest of the stars walking around her) because of his impeccable and extraordinary performance in the industry as a master craftsman across all disciplines, something that no one else could dare attempt.

Brand Rajini promoted fellowship that transcended all friendly relationships. At all possible events recounted by people who have interacted with him, humility is the single outstanding Rajini trait that is remarked. That humility has been a consistent point of attraction not only for fans but for others too. Brand Rajini can be applauded for creating a distinct cult who became his admirers not just for his acting prowess and screen presence but also for his extraordinary humility.

FUN AS A LIFESTYLE

Escape from the routine is in the spectrum of everyone's life. Having fun is the easiest and cheapest form of that escape. Having fun is a great desire too. What was escapism yesterday is a lifestyle today. Brands are finding ways and means to embed fun elements in their products or services. Brand Rajini provides a perfect space for the same for different segments of film viewers:

- For the average person who watches films as a means to escape the dreariness of daily life, Brand Rajini offers guaranteed fun.

- For the person who watches films as his or her main source of entertainment, differentiation from the average film is important, and Brand Rajini offers guaranteed differentiation.

- For the next strata, people who are Rajini fans, it is about his class, his actions and his entire repertoire. They may critique him, offer opinions on how some things could have been bettered, but they form the core of the cult. For them, you can't beat the fun they get out of a Rajini film.

- At the highest level is the Rajini madness embedded in people's emotions. They are fanatical (not in a destructive but a benign way), they swoon, they cry, they laugh and they energize with Rajini. For many of them, anything they do other than earning a living is about Rajini.

Rajini as a cult brand is always about fun. Brand Rajini makes its fans happy, cheers them up. Brand Rajini does everything that provides an escape and enjoyment in making it part of their lifestyle.

PERSONAL TRAITS

Brand Rajini uses the cult to promote the brand and attract newer, younger customers into the field of influence. This is a typical agenda. Other salient features that ensured Brand Rajini remain a cult brand stems from personal traits.

- Being accessible: Although Brand Rajini presents an expensive and legendary image, with dollops of mystery attached, most people admit that Rajini, as a person, is very accessible. This distinct feature enables Brand Rajini to build a special bond with a wide range of followers.

- Implied secret experience: The problem with popularity is a brash tongue, a 'been there, done that' attitude. Brand Rajini always presents a simple, quiet and, on many occasions, a silent demeanour. Rajini distinguished very clearly what he knew from what others thought he knew.

- Remaining calm: People in power or popularity present a sharp change in their emotional state, sometimes extending to an angered state, demonstrating a lack of control. Brand Rajini always presents an unshakable aura of calmness about him, perhaps depicting that everything is happening just as he knew it would.

- Detached involvement: Power, popularity and authority sometimes result in developing an attitude of being involved in matters that are not someone's core competence. Rajini always positioned himself as though he was above all and in a higher plane.

- Confidence, confidence and confidence: Power and popularity also breed arrogance. However, Rajini was never considered arrogant in his entire career. Confidence has been his chief trait.

Brand Equity Value

A brand is valued by the revenues it generates, the profits it makes and the goodwill it brings in. Brand equity valuation models are aplenty. That is outside the scope of this book. But how do you value a cult brand? What value can we give Brand Rajini—a super brand, an archetypal, emotional brand and a cult brand? Is it the gate collections of all his 150-plus films in current financial value? Or the current costs of all his films produced to date? A multiplier value applied to the number of times his films are seen by the approximate numbers in the Rajini cult? Can we give a valuation to the intrinsic beliefs, emotions, desires, enjoyment, fun and frolic that people feel when watching a Rajini film? There is no brand value measurement that can gauge the emotion in the bottom of your heart.

Brand Rajini will remain an unvalued brand—for we cannot give a financial value to the cherished memories of his fans, both current and future. Brand Rajini will perhaps be the most 'alive' brand to attract mankind for the years to come.

THE TOP BRANDS

Interbrands publishes lists of the most valuable brands every year. Presented below are the top twenty-five of the world's 100 best brands published for 2011. It figures the world's best brands, the best of companies having the best of products, and brand value which is probably more than its financial assets reflected in its books. From a consumer's view point, the category of the brand may vary—from emerging to power, from super to emotional, from iconic to cult.

Rank	Brand	Value (US$ Billion)
1	Coca-Cola	71.86
2	IBM	69.90
3	Microsoft	59.09
4	Google	55.31
5	GE	42.81
6	McDonald's	35.95
7	Intel	35.22
8	Apple	33.49
9	Disney	29.02
10	Hewlett Packard	28.48
11	Toyota	27.79
12	Mercedes-Benz	27.45
13	CISCO	25.31
14	Nokia	25.02
15	BMW	24.55
16	Gillette	23.99
17	Samsung	23.43
18	Louis Vuitton	23.17
19	Honda	19.43
20	Oracle	17.26
21	H&M	16.46
22	Pepsi	14.59
23	American Express	14.58
24	SAP	14.54
25	Nike	14.53

It was not a surprise that Rajini was given the NDTV Entertainer of the Decade award in 2011 (in 2007, he was crowned the Entertainer of the Year by the same channel). Though Rajini was also honoured with a few other awards—including the prestigious third-highest Indian civilian honour, the Padma Bhushan, in 2000, and the rating by Forbes India as the Most Influential Indian of the Year in 2010—the Entertainer of the Decade award most aptly communicates what Brand Rajini is all about in terms of meeting customers' expectations.

Brand Rajini can indeed stake claim as the biggest and most successful 'entertainer' in Indian cinema. An entertainer is the sum total of a person's capability and his cult following and—to borrow Raymond's tagline—Brand Rajini represents 'A complete man'.

Rajini the Cult Brand—Takeaways

Have a cause	A cult brand has a strong cause—a reason for its existence that goes beyond money. That cause makes a strong association with the beliefs of a cross-section of people who are attracted to the brand, creating a cult.
Have strong beliefs	Cult brands have strong beliefs that make a difference to the world. That differentiation leads to innovation and changes in the customers' lifestyles.

Convert your cause and belief to action	Cult brands don't just portray strong causes and beliefs; they continuously convert them into action—as reflected in their products and services.
Demonize appeal	Cult brands have to create an almost mystical appeal for their customers. They need to convert them into the brands' cheerleaders.
Design and touch	Cult brands have to design when and how people will come flocking towards the brands' offerings. The human touch should always be attached to that design to engage customer emotions, desires and beliefs.
Create a meaning	Cult brands create meaning in the lives of the brands' consumers. They provide opportunities for customers to act out their beliefs and values and they find meaning in their actions.
Belonging	Cult brands create a strong sense of belonging to the group or the cult. Their togetherness is because of the brand and the brand alone.
Leading	Cult brand creators and inventors have to lead—not the people in their group but the influence the brand has in the minds of its customers. They need to think through their actions and bring changes in the customers' mindset.

7

Brand Rajini Tomorrow

Resurrection Three

Brand Rajini had to resurrect itself once more in 2011. In 1979, *Dharma Yuddam* rescued the brand from disappearing from the industry. In 2002 too, *Baba* could have turned the brand into a failed one, and recovery was risky as well as difficult. Now, for the third time, Brand Rajini was going through a crisis.

A physical ailment occurred during the shooting of an intended period film called *Rana*. In April 2011, Rajini fell ill and was admitted to the hospital a few times in quick succession. There were plenty of rumours that shook not just the fans but also many others. Rajini was taken to Singapore for advanced treatment, and even as he was undergoing treatment, pandemonium broke out and there had to be rumour control from the family saying that all was well with Rajini. *Rana* was shelved. But Rajini resurrected like a phoenix for the third time, with a new project titled *Kochadaiyaan*. To the cult, the continued prayers offered for Rajini's well-being were answered—their love for their hero had not failed. The stills of *Kochadaiyaan* reassured everyone that Brand Rajini was ready for its next avatar.

What next for Brand Rajini? It has been an arduous but splendid journey that took Brand Rajini from a non-existent launch to becoming an established brand, and from being a power brand to an iconic and cult brand. Brand Rajini emotionally touched millions of followers. At best, Brand Rajini will be an ambassador brand for the industry and the country and it is the fervent hope of the unswerving followers of the brand that it continues to give them enriching lifestyle experiences. The task ahead for Brand Rajini is onerous: Brand Rajini will compete with Brand Rajini itself. Statistics and breaking records will not be relevant any more. The followers will continue their tryst with Brand Rajini unto eternity. And Brand Rajini, in order to give that sustained experience, may include one or more of the following brand strategies.

Humanizing Technology

The first step Brand Rajini has taken is the adoption of 'performance capturing' technology used in the likes of *Avataar* for *Kochadaiyaan*. Much like a Facebook that connects people through social networking, a Google that provides a one-stop human-web interface or a Microsoft that offers users an umbrella platform for desktop, network and cell computing, Brand Rajini is integrating available technology with human elements in order to create a completely new offering. How is the marriage between technology and Brand Rajini's offering of a lifestyle experience in *Kochadaiyaan* going to be will perhaps be the next topic of debate for his fans, followers and critics.

For a cult brand, it is not about success or failure any more, it is just about *being*.

Differentiation Is Vital

The hallmark of Brand Rajini is the continued style differentiation, from creating first impressions in *Moondru Mudichu* and *Avargal* almost four decades ago to *Enthiran* only two years ago. That differentiation will perhaps continue to compete with other brands which are capturing the mind-space of the audience, young and old. With Indian films getting globalized further, the market continues to expand and is enormous with varied customer reactions and expectations. Brand Rajini's creations have to continuously innovate in order to continue offering that cutting-edge differentiation.

Collaboration

Brand Rajini has succeeded through collaboration with the best of the creative minds in the industry—screenplay writers, cinematographers, musicians and dialogue writers and teams that ensure the delivery of the Brand Rajini experience. Brand Rajini has to make careful and concerted choices in the selection of these teams. With the passage of time, the kind of teams that will create innovative presentations focusing on Brand Rajini may dwindle as they may shift focus to popular business trends in the industry. Starting a Rajini film, with the requirements of its size, depth and reach, can be a tall order for many, who may give up at the first instance. Those who still believe in the assurance of guaranteed success in a Rajini venture may have to withstand the onslaught of multiple review mechanisms for the project to kick off. Yet, collaboration and team effort are the possible mechanisms that will be deployed for sustained success.

Simple Character, Complex Challenges

A Rajini film will continue to be centred on that simple character whom the audience can easily relate to, the one who evokes their emotions and inspires their passions. However, the challenges that the character will undergo may be complex. Those complexities may be in the context of the current environment country-specific or global events, or simply based around mythology or history. But the thread of Brand Rajini's simplicity has to be retained forever.

Back to the Basics: Connecting with the Consumer

The basic elements of a Rajini film and Brand Rajini—the clarity of thought that is portrayed, the humility that comes from within, the commitment to deliver, the responsiveness in providing innovative offerings that are relevant to the consuming public, the authenticity of the brand, its consistency of quality, its continuity of presence—will have to be explicitly seen, felt and experienced by Brand Rajini's cult. It is that which will maintain the connect.

So, What Is a Brand?

We have now rummaged through all manner of terms and definitions, from conceptual theory to actual practice, the tipping points, the good and the bad in what makes a brand. But, at the end, we need to ask ourselves in a very rudimentary way: what is a brand? When we remember an object or a feeling, can we associate a brand name with it? The answer is that sometimes we can. Consider the following examples.

If it is...

- an animated movie, it's Disney;
- an antiseptic solution, it's Dettol;
- a bandage, it's Band-Aid;
- chocolate, it's Cadbury;
- chicken on the go, it's KFC;

- coffee, it's Nescafe;
- a computer chip, it's Intel;
- a credit card, it's Visa;
- fast food, it's McDonald's;
- a handheld tablet, it's iPad;
- ketchup, it's Heinz;
- a luxury watch, it's Rolex;
- a men's magazine, it's *Playboy*;
- mainframe, it's IBM;
- noodles, it's Maggi;
- photocopy, it's Xerox;
- pizza, it's Pizza Hut;
- a portable music player, it's iPod;
- a premium car, it's Mercedes;
- a razor, it's Gillette;
- a search engine, it's Google;
- software, it's Microsoft;
- sound, it's Bose;
- sports in action, it's ESPN;
- steel, it's Tata;
- tennis, it's Wimbledon;
- tissue paper, it's Kleenex.

And we proudly conclude: if it is entertainment, it's our Grand Brand Rajini!

Acknowledgements

No words can describe our gratitude to a host of people who encouraged us to complete the book, right from its conception. We acknowledge with utmost humility the valuable contributions made by the following:

- All the people in the film industry and media and all Rajini fans across the globe who have contributed in different degrees in building, shaping, nurturing and glorifying Grand Brand Rajini.

- The publishing team at Rupa Publications, for giving us a window of opportunity to showcase Grand Brand Rajini. Special thanks to the book's commissioning editor, Ms Pradipta Sarkar, for her understanding and appreciation of the subject.

- Our families, especially our wives—Mrs Sunita Balasubraminan and Mrs Lata Ramakrishnan—for painstakingly performing the initial reviews and dotting the i's and crossing the t's.

- Anupama Ramakrishnan (student at University of Washington, Seattle), Arjun Balasubramanian (student at National Institute of Technology, Trichy), for sharing their Gen Y view of Brand Rajini. Master Jayanth Balasubramanian, a class five student, for sharing his fondness and his feedback about why Rajini is fascinating for people his age.

- An enthusiastic chartered accountants' fraternity, who gave their insight and feedback on the drafts of the book, including:

  - Mr K. A. Srinivasan (CFO, Venture East, India) and Mr K. Srinivasan (Partner, PriceWaterhouse Coopers, UAE);

  - Ms Jayasree Srinivasan and Mr P. Sankararaman of Matrix Business Services.

- Mr Suresh Narayan (Founder and Director, Quantum Leap Consulting, India), for his reviews from a marketing and branding perspective.

- To the entire NPL—Neyveli Premier League—clan; a set of friends, including us, converge at Neyveli each year (for the last twelve years) and have plenty of fun, including a two-day game of cricket. People travel from the USA, Curaçao, Hong Kong and from a few cities in India. Rajini is invariably a subject that is not missed during this confluence each year!

- Firebrand Labs, for its professional services in social media communication for this book.

Bibliography

Both of us hail from the accounting profession. For us, brand management exposure and knowledge came from our twenty-five years of corporate experience. Yet we owe a deep sense of gratitude to the many learned authors whose publications enabled us to quench our thirst for knowledge about brands, branding and brand management. We present a select list we have constantly referred to for developing this book.

- *The 22 Immutable Laws of Branding* by Al Ries and Laura Ries, New York: Harper Collins, 2002.

- *B2B Brand Management* by Phillip Kotler and Waldemar Pfoertsch, Heidelberg: Springer Berlin, 2006.

- 'Best Global Brands', Interbrands Report, 2011.

- *The Brand Bubble: The Looming Crisis in Brand Value*

and How to Avoid It by John Gerzema and Ed Lebar, San Francisco: Jossey-Bass, 2008.

- *Brand Failures* by Matt Haig, London: Kogan Page, 2003.

- *Brand Leadership: The Next Level in the Brand Revolution*, New York: The Free Press, 1996.

- *Brand Planning* by Kevin Lane Keller, Shoulder of Giants, 2009.

- *Brand Portfolio Strategy* by David A. Aaker, New York: The Free Press, 2004.

- *Brand Relevance: Making Competitors Irrelevant* by David A. Aaker, San Franciso: Jossey-Bass, 2011.

- *Brand Royalty: How the World's 100 Best Brands Thrive and Survive* by Matt Haig, London: Kogan Page, 2006.

- *BRANDCHILD: Insights into the Minds of Today's Global Kids* by Martin Lindstorm and Patricia B. Seybold, London: Kogan Page, 2003.

- *Building Strong Brands* by David A. Aaker, New York: The Free Press, 1996.

- *The Complete Idiot's Guide to Brand Management* by

Patricia F. Nicolino, Pearson, 2001.

- 'Dimensions of Brand Personality' by Jennifer Aaker, in *Journal of Marketing Research*, 1997.

- *Emotional Branding* by Marc Gobe, New York: Allworth Press, 2009.

- *The Essential Brand Book: Over 100 Techniques to Increase Brand Value* by Iain Ellwood, London: Kogan Page, 2002.

- *Global Brand Integrity Management* by Richard S. Post and Penelope N. Post, New York: McGraw-Hill, 2008.

- 'Great Brands of Tomorrow', Credit Suisse Research Institute Report, 2010.

- *Growing the Core* by David Taylor, Shoulder of Giants, 2009.

- *Harvard Business Review on Brand Management*, Review Paperback Series, HBS Press, 1999.

- *The Hero and the Outlaw: Building Extraordinary Brands through the Power of Archetypes* by Margaret Mark and Carol Pearson, New York: McGraw-Hill, 2001.

- *Managing Brand Equity* by David A. Aaker, New York: The Free Press, 1991.

- *New Strategic Brand Management* by J. N. Kapferer, London: Kogan Page, 2008.

- *A New Brand Day* by Scott Bedbury, New York: Penguin/Viking, 2002.

- *The Philosophy of Branding: Great Philosophers Think Brands* by Thom Braun, London: Kogan Page, 2004.

- *Power Branding: Building Technology Brands for Competitive Advantage* by Marty Brandt and Grant Johnson, San Francisco: International Data Group, 1997.

- *The Power of Cult Branding* by Matthew W. Ragas and Bolivar J. Bueno, New York: Prima Publishing, 2002.

- *Strategic Brand Management* by Kevin Lane Keller, Pearson Education, 2002.

- *World Famous: How to Give Your Business a Kick-Ass Brand Identity* by David Tyreman, AMACOM, 2009.

We are also grateful to the unlimited supply of information on Wikipedia as well as a number of websites, blogs and media articles that helped us compile the brand examples described in this book.

While we have taken care and caution in reporting the facts about Rajinikanth's career and the case studies cited in this book, pardon us if there have been some errors anywhere.